THE
REVOLUTIONARY
ART OF CHANGING
YOUR HEART

Also by Andrew Fuller

Tricky People
Tricky Kids
Unlocking Your Child's Genius
Life: A Guide

THE REVOLUTIONARY ART OF CHANGING YOUR HEART

An essential guide to recharging your relationship

ANDREW FULLER

First published in Australia and New Zealand in 2019
by Hachette Australia Pty Ltd

First published in Great Britain in 2019
by Headline Home
an imprint of Headline Publishing Group

1

Cataloguing in Publication Data is available from the British Library

ISBN 978 1 4722 6306 3
eISBN 978 1 4722 6305 6

Author photograph courtesy of Ponch Hawkes
Text design by Kirby Jones
Typeset in Adobe Garamond Pro by Kirby Jones

Printed and bound in Great Britain by Clays Ltd, Elcograf S.p.A.

Headline's policy is to use papers that are natural, renewable and recyclable products
and made from wood grown in sustainable forests. The logging and manufacturing processes
are expected to conform to the environmental regulations of the country of origin.

HEADLINE PUBLISHING GROUP
An Hachette UK Company
Carmelite House
50 Victoria Embankment
London EC4Y 0DZ

www.headline.co.uk
www.hachette.co.uk

For Vicki,

who makes my eyes smile and my heart sing

CONTENTS

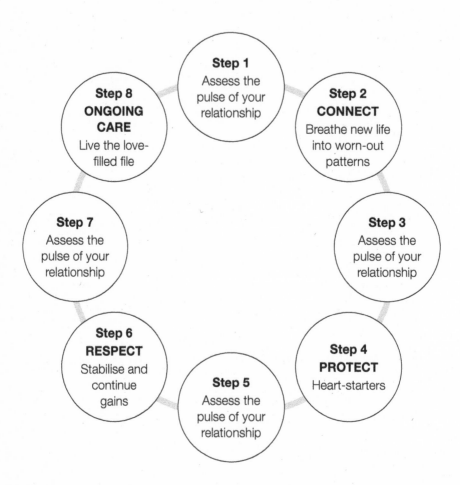

CPR model: Connect, protect and respect

AS YOU LOVE, SO YOU WILL BE

Love puts magic in your eyes – it makes them smile. Whether your eyes are smiling at the moment or have been dimmed by sadness, this book will help you make a revolutionary change in your life and relationships.

Whether you are building a great relationship, or saving one that has fallen on tough times, or are mending your heartbreak before starting anew, this book will gently guide you towards making this revolutionary change.

The following chapters outline how to provide 'CPR' for relationships. I have developed this approach over 35 years as a psychology professional, working with individuals, couples and families at all stages of life. Extensive research has shown me that relationships function best and people thrive together when they:[1]

Connect

Protect *and*

Respect

When we connect, protect and respect each other we can create good relationships and heal troubled ones. Unless we breathe new life into a relationship it will dwindle and perish. If your relationship has hit a rocky patch, this is the time to be honest enough to admit that the ways you and your partner have related in the past haven't worked as well as they needed to.

Not changing doesn't necessarily mean separating, but unless you undergo some change, at least two people are likely to be incredibly unhappy. This is why I have developed my CPR techniques to save relationships. Just as with CPR in emergencies, there are rarely second chances.

The best relationships of your life are ahead of you – because *The Revolutionary Art of Changing Your Heart* will help you to create the best relationships of your life.

Outlined on the next few pages are the revolutionary steps you will take. If you can commit to these steps, the benefits you will receive will be life changing.

Step 1 – Assess the pulse of your relationship

First, check for signs of life and ensure that it is safe for you to start to resuscitate your relationship. This involves feeling confident that there is sufficient pulse to make engaging in CPR a worthwhile process. If there is a history of violence or abuse in your relationship, read the Appendix, 'Dealing with Dangerous Relationships', before beginning CPR.

Step 2 – Connect: Breathe new life into worn-out patterns – 'linking and syncing'

Step two involves looking for ways to connect. This is about 'linking and syncing' between you and your partner. You need to know what you want and what it is about yourself that will help you to create a great relationship. Then you need to connect with your partner and know how they can be with you to create a love that is fulfilling and fun.

Step 3 – Assess the pulse of your relationship

Time again to assess the state of your relationship before moving to the next stage.

Step 4 – Protect: Heart-starters for a better relationship and a better way of being

This next stage, Protect, is where things really change. This is where you put into place the heart-starters for a better relationship and a better way of being. Your fledgling hopes and dreams need to be protected as you build trust, hope and intimacy.

Step 5 – Assess the pulse of your relationship

Time again to assess the state of your relationship before moving to the next stage.

Step 6 – Respect: Stabilise and continue gains

The next stage is Respect. The gains you've made can be so easily swept aside in a moment of heated argument, doubt or distrust. You will find ways to respect yourself and your partner, to have your lives, your loves and your hearts sing in harmony.

Step 7 – Assess the pulse of your relationship

Time again to assess the state of your relationship before moving to the next stage.

Step 8 – Ongoing care: Live the love-filled life

The eighth stage is ongoing care – making sure you live a love-filled life. This is where you make the revolutionary gains you have made part of your everyday life so you can have a great partnership together.

This is a book to read slowly. Implement the ideas and strategies gradually – the CPR methods are powerful and you need time to entwine them into your relationship. As a rule of thumb, I suggest implementing this approach over two to three months.

Now it's time to start! It's time to embrace the challenges and reap the rewards of the revolutionary art of changing your heart.

PART ONE

THE EIGHT-STEP RELATIONSHIP RECHARGE

ASSESS THE PULSE OF YOUR RELATIONSHIP

Before applying CPR to resuscitating and renewing your relationship, it's essential that you are safe. Change can unsettle relationships. Not all partners appreciate it when the people they are with become empowered or more free. Some can feel threatened. Consider whether you feel safe enough to make some improvements without risking damage to yourself or to your partner.

If you feel at all doubtful, read the Appendix, 'Dealing with Dangerous Relationships'. Discuss the pros and cons of making changes with trusted friends or professionals. Ask them whether they can foresee any issues or problems that may be invisible to you. It can be hard to see a relationship clearly when you are in it.

Assuming you feel safe to implement some changes, let's begin. The first step is to consider whether your relationship is:

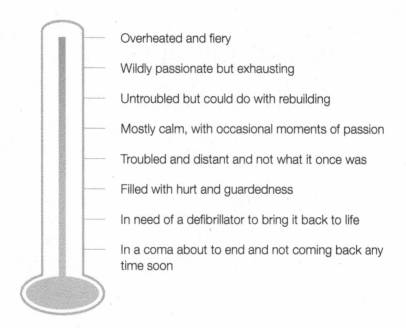

Overheated and fiery

Wildly passionate but exhausting

Untroubled but could do with rebuilding

Mostly calm, with occasional moments of passion

Troubled and distant and not what it once was

Filled with hurt and guardedness

In need of a defibrillator to bring it back to life

In a coma about to end and not coming back any time soon

If you are feeling heartbroken you may first wish to read the Breakup Recovery Guide in Part Two before beginning CPR.

Even if your relationship is 100 per cent dead and there seems to be nothing you can do, the CPR method will help you. Finetuning our abilities to link and sync with others is how we all begin to connect.

Several times throughout the book you will be asked to assess the state of your relationship like this. This is because honesty with yourself is the starting point for change. It is also useful to monitor your progress as you implement CPR.

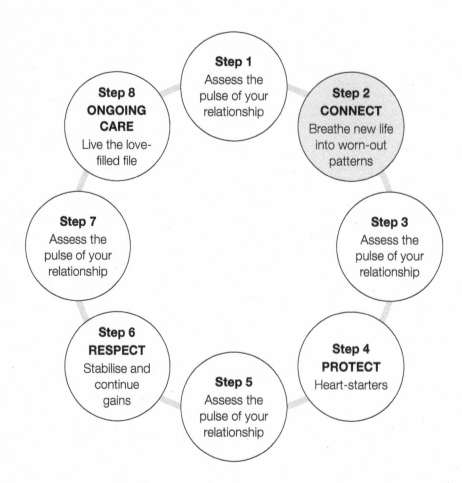

CPR model: Connect, protect and respect

CONNECT
BREATHE NEW LIFE INTO WORN-OUT PATTERNS – LINKING AND SYNCING

Let's prepare a gift for you right now and also for your great, great, great, great, great grandson or granddaughter, a gift that will continue to be delivered in the year 2320. This gift is the ability to form and maintain secure, happy relationships.

Connect to yourself

Before connecting with other people, spend some time connecting with yourself. As you work through this section, it is always tempting to ask yourself, 'Is this part of me good or bad?', 'Should I be this way or some other way?' While it is natural and healthy to think like this, it is also important to realise that being you is enough. There is a sign in my psychology practice that says:

BE YOURSELF

EVERYONE ELSE IS TAKEN

THEY ARE ALL FULL OF BEING THEMSELVES

Being who you are, knowing who you are and what you want, then knowing how to create it, is the purpose of this section. It is not about judging one way as better or worse than another.

As humans we have all inherited stories and styles from our relatives and ancestors about how to run our relationships. Some of these stories have great strengths but they also have a few weak points, especially when we feel threatened or under stress. These stories give us choices about how we act and react.

Before you criticise your own history of relationship patterns harshly, consider that they also must have a positive side. If you want proof of this, consider for a moment the odds against your existence, which are roughly one in 400 trillion.

By the way, the chances of you existing at all are less than the chance that there is another liveable planet like Earth out there. So let's thank our ancestors – even if they have given us some interesting relationship styles – and get on with it!

What type of partner are you?

First up is a quiz to determine what kind of partner you are in a relationship. Give yourself 2 points for each true answer, 1 point for maybe and 0 points for false.

1.	I become best friends with my partners	True	Maybe	False
2.	I always believe my relationships will be permanent	True	Maybe	False
3.	I find routine home activities to be comfortable and relaxing	True	Maybe	False
4.	I accept that short separations from my lover are just a part of life	True	Maybe	False
5.	I can't remember really falling in love, it was more like I had been in love for some time without realising it	True	Maybe	False
		Score		

6.	I am forgiving in my relationships	True	Maybe	False
7.	I would excuse my loved one for anything	True	Maybe	False
8.	Rather than falling in love, I am just a loving person	True	Maybe	False
9.	I would wait for my partner to be released from prison or from a psychiatric hospital	True	Maybe	False
10.	I am a loyal, supportive person	True	Maybe	False
		Score		

11.	I have peaks of excitement in love but also depths of despair	True	Maybe	False
12.	I can get really jealous	True	Maybe	False
13.	I am highly anxious in relationships	True	Maybe	False
14.	I do not tolerate short times away from my lover well	True	Maybe	False
15.	At times I worry I might become a burden to others	True	Maybe	False
		Score		

16.	I look for a partner who matches my social standing, earning capacity and ambitions	True	Maybe	False
17.	I am loyal and faithful	True	Maybe	False
18.	I am loyal but if my partner became ill or they lost their job I would reconsider the relationship	True	Maybe	False
19.	I help my partner realise their potential and advance themselves	True	Maybe	False
20.	If we broke up I would only separate at a time that suited me	True	Maybe	False
		Score		

21.	I hate feeling dependent	True	Maybe	False
22.	When dating, I keep several potential lovers on the string	True	Maybe	False
23.	I would prefer to find a new sex partner than work out problems with an existing one	True	Maybe	False
24.	I don't like commitment	True	Maybe	False
25.	I want a partner who is not demanding	True	Maybe	False
		Score		

26.	I believe in love at first sight	True	Maybe	False
27.	I can remember exactly the details of the first moment I met my lover	True	Maybe	False
28.	Anniversaries are important to me	True	Maybe	False
29.	In a relationship I would like to wear matching clothes or rings	True	Maybe	False
30.	I search for new ways to please my lover	True	Maybe	False
		Score		

While you will be a mix of types it is useful to think about your main one or two types. If you scored highest on:

- questions 1–5, you are a soulmate
- questions 6–10, you are devoted
- questions 11–15, you are wildly romantic
- questions 16–20, you are a cool calculator
- questions 21–25, you are commitment phobic
- questions 26–30, you are a true romantic.

1. Soulmate

You like your partners to be good friends who develop into intimate partners over time. You might suddenly realise the friend you have been spending so much time with is actually the person you love. You believe relationships are permanent and together you will find a way to deal with any problems that arise.

Once you are in a relationship, you don't search for new lovers or new love experiences. You enjoy the security of being settled in a relationship in which each person is able to predict the other's responses to their behaviours.

A relationship between two soulmates is like having another person ingrained into your being. Temporary separations are not a great problem for you. You will miss your partner but you don't mistrust them. Passion and sex can be deeply intimate and satisfying.

Some people fall in love; you fall into loving togetherness with people and then recognise that you are in love.

Anniversaries and birthdays are often not important to you because life is a cause for continual celebration. Conflicts, when they do occur, are not a sign that you do not love each other. They are troubling in that you want to get back to the closeness of togetherness as quickly as possible. Should you ever separate or break up, you would probably remain close friends, actively caring about one another.

Both Carole King and James Taylor sang 'You've Got a Friend' – they could have been singing your theme song.

2. Devoted

You are so forgiving that it bewilders some of your friends. When someone wrongs you, your first inclination is to dismiss it as a mistake or to see it as a sign that they are a victim of forces beyond their control.

You don't so much fall in love as exude it out of the pores of your skin. The happiness of others matters to you. You care for animals, the helpless and the vulnerable, and still have a special place in your heart for your own loved ones. For those people there ain't no mountain high enough, ain't no river wide enough to keep you from loving them.

However, your patience teeters on the brink of masochism. Once you have decided who you want to be in a relationship with, you stay. You will put up with a lot to preserve that relationship and will work hard to ensure its success, which is why at times you will need the CPR methods.

Now before we put up statues in your honour and suggest that you should be a candidate for sainthood, there are a few downsides to mention. You are always supportive of your partner but the risk is that of any muse to a creative spirit: you may eventually feel bitter or overlooked. If the relationship ends, you may feel so deeply hurt and devastated that you won't know how to go on. It is not that you give too much, it is that you need reminding to give as much to yourself as you do to your lover.

A relationship between two devotees is a life of mutual admiration. Children in families with two devotee parents may complain that their parents loved each other so much there wasn't room for them.

'My Baby Just Cares for Me' by Nina Simone; 'I Would Die 4 U' by Prince; 'Fall at Your Feet' by Crowded House; 'Hopelessly Devoted to You' from *Grease*; and the Bill Withers song 'Use Me' could serve as your theme songs.

3. Wildly romantic

You are obsessed with your lover. You could eat them for breakfast, lunch and dinner. Well, not literally, but you get the gist. You may be unable to sleep, eat or even think logically around them. There is not much stability in your romantic life. You have the peaks of excitement and the depths of despair with not much calm between.

Can you be jealous? Do bears live in the woods? You grow jealous very easily. You find it hard to be out of contact with your lover, even for short periods of time. Your mobile phone is both a blessing and a curse. If your partner is out of contact or doesn't answer a call from you, you can be consumed with fears of betrayal or feelings of rejection.

You can be changeable. One moment you may suggest spending a few days apart to think about things and then in the middle of the night go into a panic because you can't locate your partner. You don't easily tolerate being apart for extended periods.

If you can't learn to calm yourself you may also become prone to anxiety-related health issues including sexual problems such as vaginismus or premature ejaculation. You may also be prone to fears that there are younger and more attractive versions of yourself around. This may lead to a fear of getting older and also lead to an endless shopping trip trying to find 'the one'.

Relationships involving two wildly romantic people are preoccupying for both, with short periods of calm between lengthy periods of either wild passion or nail-scratching intensity.

The songs 'Losing My Mind' by Stephen Sondheim; 'Night and Day' by Cole Porter; or 'Need Ur Luv' by Charlie XCX could be themes for you.

4. Cool calculator

It is likely that you have a checklist of criteria for potential partners and if someone doesn't tick all your boxes, it's not happening anytime soon. For you, relationships are an investment to be made carefully. Once the 'deal' is made, you remain loyal and faithful and define yourself as 'in a relationship'. Should the circumstances or assets of your partner change, you may feel that the contract has been violated and begin to search for another partner. You will give a lot of yourself to have your partner succeed in life. Their success is your success. You might support them while they complete a course, or coach them to ask for a pay rise or promotion at work. You also look after them by ensuring they receive the attention they deserve – for example, from doctors, friends and employers.

Your meet-ups are part date, part interrogation. You might check out future in-laws and friends and ascertain the likelihood of inherited defects in your future children.

Relationships between two cool calculators are like investments in a shared business and the costs of quitting can outweigh other potential pleasures. If you break up, it will be for practical reasons. Divorce may be planned for some future date. For example, you may decide to put your youngest child through high school before getting divorced.

You think ahead about family size (and probably even about what sex the children will be), career prospects and finances. Your theme songs are 'Hearts Don't Break Around Here' by Ed Sheeran; 'Please Please Me' by the Beatles; 'Under My Thumb' by the Rolling Stones; and 'Smooth Operator' by Sade.

5. Commitment phobic

You don't like commitment. You don't like people who take you for granted. You dislike clinginess and dependency, either in yourself or in others. Every so often you surprise yourself by being romantic and at times even clingy (for brief, intense periods that you often don't want to talk about afterwards).

Intimacy is usually partial with you. There are things you will share and things you will not. You may be hard to really get to know.

At times you may have 'insurance' partners, keeping several lovers or potential lovers on the go at one time. Generally you would rather find a new sex partner than to work out sexual problems with an existing one.

With past loves you may suddenly swoop in years later with birthday flowers, a bottle of a favourite wine, a sentimental gift – only to vanish just as suddenly.

You enjoy love affairs and rarely regret them unless the threat of dependency becomes too great. Dates with you are fun, even though they may be infrequent and your prevaricating ambivalence may test the patience of even the most determined and desirous of your partners.

As a rule, you have one main sexual repertoire and if your partner is not pleased you simply move on to someone else. Sex is more biological than emotional.

Relationships between two commitment phobes are a fine balancing act. Both have to be similarly unavailable to be attractive to the other; each coming together has to feel like a conquest against the odds. This often suits people who frequently travel separately for work, people on different shifts or people who like to spend most of their time alone or with family and friends.

Your songs are 'Don't Fence Me In' by Bing Crosby and the Andrews Sisters; 'Same Old Love' by Selena Gomez; 'How to Love' by Lil Wayne; and Bob Dylan's 'All I Really Want to Do'.

6. True romantic

You are a romantic. You believe in love at first sight. For you, falling in love has all the bells and whistles – the stars twinkle at night, the birds sing sweetly and all is well in your world.

You remember exactly how your partner looked when you first set eyes upon them. You remember exactly the day you met, your first kiss and everything about your first sexual experience together. You expect your partners to share these memories vividly and feel disappointed if they don't.

You always try to look your best. You won't risk losing your lover's admiration. You seek out new ways to please them – gifts, new foods and new sexual techniques.

When love strikes you, it is hard, fast and complete. You don't just fall in love, you immerse yourself in it. You want to know everything about your partner from the first moment you meet them – all of their experiences, joys and sorrows. You want to tell and share everything with them.

At times you feel you would like to merge, so much so that you could become one person. You may like to wear similar clothes and order the same foods when dining out, and be identified with your lover as much as possible. You are rarely apart from your lover, so jealousy is not often an issue. There is thorough commitment.

Relationships between two romantics are often of the 'mate once, mate for life' variety, so if problems arise they are deeply troubling and hard to mend. Break-ups are explosive, shattering and painful.

Your theme songs are 'Total Control' by The Motels; 'Hands to Myself' by Selena Gomez; Joni Mitchell's 'All I Want'; Prince's 'Anotherloverholenyohead'; Blondie's 'One Way or Another'; 'I Knew I Loved You' by Savage Garden; and 'Just Give Me a Reason' by Pink.

Know what you are looking for

You may want to pause here and think about what or who you want in a relationship. First, think about the type of lover that you are. Then think about the type of lover your partner is.

Be careful. It is too easy to see yourself as a soulmate, wildly romantic or totally devoted while they are cool calculators or commitment phobes. This might be the case but just double-check on yourself to see whether you are being fair.

Then it is worth thinking about what you are looking for:

- A 'bad' boy or girl to have fun with?
- Someone you can shape a successful career and life with?
- A life partner?
- An adventurer into the wild frontiers of life?
- A parent for future children?
- A parent for yourself?
- Someone who will totally love you but conveniently go away when you want them to?
- Someone by your side as an ally?
- Someone who can help you repair your own upbringing?
- Someone you can look after and maybe even repair a bit?
- A passionate wildly sexual being who leaves you gasping and sleep deprived?
- Someone who will make you look smarter, funnier and even more good-looking?
- Someone safe?

You may want a combination of these characteristics. Think about the two or three features that are most important to you.

Understanding attraction

With the exception of family members, it's no accident that we end up in relationships with most of the people in our lives. It is a matter of choice. Either you choose them or they choose you or you choose each another.

Relationships are healthiest when they are based on continual choosing because to keep actively choosing to be with the people you are with is a powerful way of connecting.

Even if you airily say that you and your friend/manager/business partner/lover/husband/wife met at a party and something 'just clicked', let's look at what caused that click to occur. What starts most relationships, including friendships, is attraction. Understanding attraction is important. Attraction is not just physical. For example, if you met your partner in a work setting, you were attracted to the idea of working there in the first place.

Attraction is not a matter of accident, but it's not just a matter of conscious choice either. Often our early love choices are based on similarity – we grew up in the same area, went to school together, knew the same people or worked together. If you think about it, the accident of being co-located is a fairly poor basis for choosing a life partner. Despite this, it can work out well for some people.

Another pathway to attraction is to become attracted to people who *appear* to have handled things that we find difficult to deal with. Part of attraction is solving a problem – we look for people who are capable in areas where we feel vulnerable. For example, a woman who grows up in a family with alcoholics may select someone who is as dry as a Methodist christening. A man who has grown up in harsh or violent circumstances may search for a partner who seems as loving and gentle as Mother Teresa.

And so then everyone should live happily ever after, right? Wrong!

The shadow self

As we grow up there are parts of ourselves that people praise and find acceptable:

- He/she's so good at ...
- I love the way you ...
- She/he's such a clever girl/boy, see how they ...
- Aren't you wonderful at ...

These are some of the phrases that indicate desirable characteristics. After being applauded for them, we feel compelled to put these characteristics on display, and make them major features of our personality. As such, they will gain us love and accolades.

We are not, however, just dancing seals performing for the next bit of fish or, in this case, praise – we also put on display parts of ourselves that we value. For almost every characteristic that we put on show, though, there are others that have not been approved of or applauded. All of us have parts of ourselves that we don't like so much. Without really thinking about it, we shove these parts under the metaphorical carpet and hide them away. After a while we become so good at this, we can even pretend that they never existed at all. The father of psychoanalysis, Carl Jung (1957), called this the 'shadow self'.[2]

Then we go out into the world in search of other people to relate to and become attracted to. Without really meaning to, we seek out other people who *appear to be* capable in the areas where we feel vulnerable. The only problem here is that what gives them the appearance of being capable is often that they have tucked away and hidden the very same stuff that we find difficult to deal with. They may even have a better cover story or disguise than the one we have.

This shadow self is not an entirely controllable beast. It slips off the leash and gets out of the cage in times of duress and stress. It loves bad hair days.

For example, someone who is attracted to a mild-mannered, placid soul may find that in difficult times this partner can become a seething vat of fury and rage. A shy, retiring person who has found a wild party gal or guy as a partner may be dismayed when they transform into a mild homebody or an absent workaholic.

This partly explains why relationships can begin with a sense that 'we have so much in common', only to find crevasses of difference later on. The people haven't actually changed, it's that their shadow selves have come out to play.

Before thinking about other people's shadows you need to acknowledge your own. Shadow selves gain power over us when we pretend they don't exist. The first step in helping yourself is to look for parts of yourself that you don't like and accept that they are there. Accepting this doesn't mean excusing yourself for every nasty, mean, sneaky, cranky thing you've done – it means acknowledging that at times you can be like this.

The philosopher Friedrich Nietzsche said that one of the best days in his life was the day when he rebaptised all his negative qualities as his best qualities.

Windows into understanding yourself and others

The Johari window provides an effective way of understanding the complexity of our selves.[3] This model suggests we are all a bit like a four-roomed building, which has four windows. One room is visible to both ourselves and others. One is visible only to us. A third can be seen only by others, and the final room can be seen by no one.

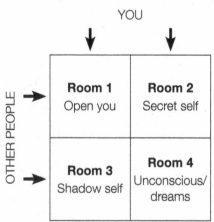

ROOM 1 IS THE OPEN YOU

This room has a window into which both you and others can see. The 'open you' comprises the parts of you that you are aware of and that other people can see. These are the aspects of you that are on show, about which you might say, 'I'm that sort of person' and other people would agree, 'Yes, you're that sort of person.'

ROOM 2 IS THE PRIVATE OR SECRET YOU

This room contains aspects of yourself that you don't readily share. It might be secret information; it might be things you don't share through modesty. It is a side of you that very few, if any, other people see. You know about these parts of you but tuck them away from the eyes of others. There is nothing wrong or damaging about doing this.

ROOM 3 IS THE SHADOW YOU

This room contains information about yourself that you aren't consciously aware of but other people can see. Scary, huh? There are things about you that other people know better than you know.

ROOM 4 IS THE UNCONSCIOUS SELF

This is the part of you that no one gets to see directly. You don't get to see it, and neither do other people. This is your unconscious, a warehouse of information that is usually only accessed through dreams.

What do you think is in each of your rooms? It is not that any of these rooms are undesirable, but increasing our awareness of them helps in forming relationships.

Learning this about ourselves is valuable. As the work of psychotherapist Carl Rogers informs us, when we accept others as they are, it frees them to change; when we learn to accept ourselves, we can begin to change too.[4]

Accepting that other people also have shadow selves that they are largely unaware of can help you to understand their behaviour, even if you don't like it. It is useful to be aware of and able to observe shadows when they arise.

In the heat of an argument it can be awfully tempting to tell someone, 'You always do X and I know exactly why! It's because you can't handle X.' Avoid doing this! People have spent years carefully assembling a self that ignores the shadow parts of themselves and if you point it out to them when they are upset or angry they will argue vehemently that you are wrong and may even become violent.

Shadow selves don't just play a role in attraction, they also impact on the fine checks and balances that play out in many relationships. For example, how much control you exert *over* others or can tolerate *from* others may be dictated by your shadow self.

What type of attachment do you create?

Think of time when you were a child and you were physically hurt. The first memory that comes to your mind is the one to use. Perhaps you fell off something, or cut yourself or were bruised in a game. Hopefully it wasn't too nasty and didn't hurt too much. What happened? How did you deal with the hurt? Who helped you?

The answers to these questions tell us more that you might realise – we'll talk more about this at the end of this chapter.

The pattern that keeps on giving

First let's think about a pattern that plays a powerful role in all of our lives. We often repeat in our relationships the way we were treated as children.

It is rare that we sit back from the rush of life and top up our early servings of love and security. Because most of us don't do this, we often repeat the past. Many of our relationships follow the same pattern over and over again. These repeating patterns could explain why you may have some adult friends who at regular intervals phone you in great drama, then tearfully visit while draining your house of alcohol as they plot how to pick up their next future ex-husband or -wife.

After a while all of our relationships begin to resemble one another. We search for happiness in new loving relationships but without an awareness of the patterns we are destined to repeat. Different person, same issues.

Our earliest relationships with our parents, grandparents and caregivers play a powerful role in the way we relate to others – they form our pattern of attachment.

Secure belonging and attachment

About 55 per cent of us have won what John Bowlby called the lottery of life.[5] We were lucky enough to have a parent, parents or caregivers who were able to do four important things for us, in addition to loving us.

First, they helped us to put words to that morass of stuff we call feelings. They would say things like, 'You seem happy today', or asked, 'Are you feeling angry about that?' or, 'Are you feeling upset about what happened?'

Second, they helped us to understand that not everyone feels the same way we do. If you're feeling upset or angry it doesn't necessarily mean that everybody else is feeling angry and upset with you. It takes a while to learn how to differentiate our own feelings from other people's feelings.

Third, they helped us to learn how to calm ourselves down. By being soothed by others when we were upset, we eventually learned to do this for ourselves.

Fourth, they helped us to learn when we felt dejected or bored or disinterested to go and do something different. They helped us to learn to come back from these times and how to resume being curious, happy and settled.

A secure attachment involves learning that you are loved and gives you a basic introduction to emotional intelligence: knowing your own feelings, identifying and sensing feelings in other people and knowing how to calm yourself down when you are upset. You learn to trust yourself and then you learn to trust other people.

Having that security goes a long way towards creating successful relationships and therefore a happy life.

How our sense of belonging can be distorted

Ideally, all of us would feel a secure sense of belonging that enables us to set up strong, positive relationships with other people. Life, however, is rarely ideal.

For some of us, our early experiences were fraught with poverty, tension, family break-up, illness, postnatal depression or just tough times. For others it was our own illnesses or our temperaments as babies that made it difficult for us to feel secure. This is not necessarily anyone's fault. While they are all unfortunate, circumstances such as these were simply facts of life at the time.

Avoidant belonging and attachment

About 25 per cent of us develop an avoidant form of attachment that means we don't really seek out or want close relationships. Our history of feeling vulnerable makes us wary and distrustful of intimacy and very close relationships.

During childhood we may become fiercely self-reliant and not let ourselves be comforted by others. Friendships may come and go, and we move on. In romantic relationships, the big question becomes, 'Can I rely on this person?' As adults, at times we may sabotage or avoid close relationships. There is a recurrent theme of, 'I can sort this out best by myself.'

You may have met adults like this in your life: people who seem to have a checklist for potential partners and then, just as someone starts ticking all the boxes they add a few more criteria, just to make sure they don't get there.

You may have met people like this, who are often capable, successful and involved in all sorts of activities and committees. They may do a lot of good in the world, some of them even becoming beloved 'aunties' and 'uncles' (as long as they can send the kids back to their homes at the end of the day), but if you sit down with them and chat about romance it becomes clear that the romantic world is a foreign land that they are not interested in visiting. If you ask them about romance, they will look at you questioningly and wonder why you would bother.

These are adults who turn away from the world of romance and close friendship, and instead devote themselves to their career, hobbies, sport or other activities. When people with avoidant attachment styles are in relationships they keep part of themselves to themselves. They prefer to soothe themselves, not talk about their worries or concerns and not deal with their vulnerabilities with their partners. Some of them may even seem to have a more involved relationship with their phone or their computer than with their partner.

There is nothing inherently wrong with this style of attachment – in fact it can have advantages. Avoidant people can display the following characteristics. They:

- are self-reliant and capable
- are not overly fazed by complexities or emotional turmoil
- are calm (at least on the outside)
- appear 'strong' to others
- are able to focus on career and other goals
- can keep away and tune out from personal dramas
- don't feel overly vulnerable
- can cope with a relatively high turnover of partners.

There are also disadvantages, though – if you're avoidant, you:

- tend to be a 'lone wolf' who can't easily ask for help from others
- can ask for help, but often indirectly through hints, complaints or sulking
- can be seen as inconsiderate, arrogant or thoughtless
- can be cynical about love
- may put too much emphasis on career success at the expense of relationship success.

Thoughts that avoidant people may have:

- 'I don't need anyone.'
- 'Don't get too involved, you'll only be disappointed.'
- 'Men won't commit to a relationship.'
- 'Women will try to trap you.'
- 'I found my partner much more attractive before we became a couple.'
- 'Why does he/she demand so much from me?'
- 'Why do you have to make such a drama out of everything?'
- 'If it wasn't for you we wouldn't have problems.'
- 'You've got to put up with a lot to stay involved with a man/woman.'
- 'There are other, more important things in life than romance.'
- 'You've got to protect yourself. You're going to get hurt in this relationship.'
- 'You're too good for him/her.'
- 'I don't mind having you in the house but do you have to be in my room as well?'

Anxious belonging and attachment

About 20 per cent of us become anxious and clingy in our relationships. Now, before you become too self-diagnostic, all of us can have bad days in our relationships. If this turns into an ongoing pattern, though, we should start to analyse ourselves.

Feeling anxiously attached makes us prone to pessimism and feeling clingy, jealous, being dependent on others and with rock-bottom self-esteem. The most common feeling is of being unworthy of love. People who are insecure often feel mystified that people want to be their friends and astonished that anyone could fall in love with them.

People with anxious attachment are often incapable of calming their fears or soothing themselves, and rely on others to help them deal with upsets. Adults in this group start romantic relationships anxiously and worry whether they are worthy of the person they are with. This can lead to panic and fears of being abandoned whenever there is distance or conflict in the relationship. Being in love is filled with anxiety but being without love is seen as unbearable.

Again, there is nothing inherently bad about this. The advantages of being anxiously attached are that:

- you are more sensitive
- you like intimacy and closeness
- you want to work to save your relationship
- you are quicker to detect threats – more sensitive alarm bells
- you get the great highs of the relationships
- you wear your heart on your sleeve
- you can take responsibility
- people know where they stand with you
- you talk things through.

The disadvantages are:

- anxiety
- over-sensitivity
- self-doubt
- sleep disturbances through worrying
- the capacity to create the very uncertainty you fear – by constantly seeking reassurance you can push people away
- insecurity
- stomach ailments, digestive problems
- always being on the lookout for problems

- headaches and stress-related conditions
- being seen by others as 'high maintenance'.

Thoughts that anxiously attached people may have:

- 'They are going to leave me.'
- 'I am not good enough for them.'
- 'If I really, really please them, they will stay with me.'
- 'Do you love me?'
- 'Do you really love me?'
- 'Yes, but do you really, really love me?'

To complicate matters, there's a much smaller group of people with anxious attachment who also appear to be avoidant. These are people who feel deeply fragile in love and create a persona of not needing people and not wanting closeness. They can act as if they are 'super-tough' or 'super-independent' and be dismissive of emotions and needs. They are often 'super-copers' who appear Teflon-coated to others; they can survive any rebuff, overlook any rejection and don't mess around with any of that romantic stuff.

For some of these people, it takes a major life event such as a life-threatening illness to break through their persona and show their vulnerabilities and anxieties. Others never do and remain brittle and isolated.

Let's look at the combinations

While we often want to place people exactly in one category or another, life is not so neat. We can all move between secure, anxious and avoidant at different times and under different circumstances. Given time we can also intentionally change our attachment style.

We will discuss this more in Step 4, in the 'The Key to Successful Relationships' section. Basically we all have a home base – secure, anxious or avoidant – but all of us can have moments when we move between these different relationship modes. The trick is knowing how to pull yourself and eventually your partner out of the anxious and avoidant states and to begin feeling secure.

The table on page 46 looks at all the possible combinations. You might be able to see yourself and the people you relate to in a number of these combinations.

	Anxious	Avoidant	Secure
Soulmate	Needs to have the other available almost all the time	Rare mix, but may find someone who can be a lifelong friend or partner	Likes closeness and can tolerate times apart
Devoted	Needs to be able to do things to please the other person	Loves from afar, adoration, 'pedestal worship', diminishment of the self	Able to love intensely and also look after themselves
Wild Romantic	Erratic, high passion flitting from loving to anger and back again	Withholds information, changes the topic, makes excuses to get away, switches off as a way of managing conflict	Loves deeply, discusses closely, resolves carefully
Cool Calculator	Conducts risk assessments, overly sensitised to warning signs, has checklists and a faulty alarm system	Is this really worth the bother? Runs hot and cold, ambivalent, looks for other options	Uses a cool head at work but a warm heart in love
Commitment Phobic	Secretly desires freedom but fears the other wants the same	Always feels trapped or stifled by the other; may overemphasise the 'sacrifices they have made'	Able to see that intimacy doesn't have to threaten independence
True Romantic	Love is in the details; tests to see whether the other loves them as much as they love	Distance equals excitement – their passion declines when too close or comfortable with the other	Finds the allure of seduction wonderful and can enjoy being in a relationship

Relationships between people with anxious and avoidant attachment styles usually take the most CPR to get right. Avoidant people often strive to keep their distance and their independence. When conflicts arise, they express their feelings less, spend less time with their romantic partners, shut down and turn their attention to other things, downplay their distress and overly rely on themselves.

Anxious people strive to be closer to their romantic partners. When conflicts arise they draw attention to their suffering, displaying heightened distress and relying on their partners for comfort and reassurance.

These opposing motivations and strategies have important implications for the functioning of both partners in the relationship. People will move around between different responses but will usually have a few main items in their repertoire.

No matter what attachment 'type' you might be, a couple of things to consider are:

- Your attachment needs are your attachment needs.
- There are great advantages in life to feeling securely attached.

Think about where you currently are on a continuum of attachment:

Avoidant	Secure	Anxious

You don't become more secure by denying your attachment needs; you become more secure by expressing your attachment needs. When you are able to ask your partner openly for what you need and you are listened to, you begin the process of trusting, which leads to feeling secure.

For example, say something like, 'Right now I am feeling a bit hemmed in. I need to be by myself to think things through for an hour or two. We will be okay. I'll be back to discuss this but I need to think it through in my own way first.' Or, 'At the moment I need to know that you are there for me, that you have my back and that our relationship is the most important thing for you. I need a hug now.'

When you were a child, hopefully you learned that your parents could leave you for short periods and then return. Gradually you became comfortable and confident that they would be back. It is much the same process for adults in a relationship. Learning to express your attachment needs and have them acted upon will give you the confidence to come back into harmony with each other.

If you feel you can have the space you need, when you need it, you are less likely to need as much space. If you can have the closeness and reassurance you need, when you need it, you are less likely to worry.

You don't become more secure by denying your attachment needs; you become more secure by expressing your attachment needs. When you are able to ask your partner openly for what you need and you are listened to, you begin the process of trusting, which leads to feeling secure.

Life lessons in love

You get what you look for

The first lesson to understand is that people get what they look for in life. You may notice this in the people you meet. People who look for betrayal in others often end up consumed with jealousy. People who look for avoidance and lack of consideration in others often end up feeling they need to be in control. People who look for anger in others often end up with feelings of fear. People who look for reassurance from others often end up with greater uncertainty. Look for the best in others and you will often get it.

Give to others what you want for yourself

The second lesson is: Give to other people what you would like to receive yourself. If you would like more playfulness in your life, you need to be playful towards other people. If you would like more love in your life, you need to be more loving to others.

Have you slipped into being a victim?

It is easy when times are tough or torrid to see ourselves as victims. Almost without realising it, we blame other people for our woes. The problem with this view is twofold: it stops us taking the necessary steps to look after ourselves, and it diminishes our contribution to our relationships.

There are two signs that you may have slipped into the disempowered territory of victimhood: first, if when people detect you are upset or not your usual self you deny the existence of any problems; second, if you find yourself using justification, blame or defensive language every time you talk about your relationship.

In all of our relationships we have four basic choices:

1. Stay in the relationship, change what can be changed and live by your values.
2. Stay, accept what can't be changed and live by your values.
3. Stay, give up and do things that make the relationship worse.
4. Leave the relationship and live by your values.

Pulse report

Before you move into action and start the process of improving your relationships, let's undertake a quick review. Given what you have thought about in terms of attachment styles and the different types of lovers, let's again take the pulse of your relationship.

At the beginning of this chapter, I asked you to remember a time in your childhood when you were hurt, and what you did. That memory can tell you a lot about yourself. The incident you remembered represents the way you deal with challenges and issues in your life. This is something you learned very early on in life and unless you have thought about it much before reading this, it continues to this day. These are your attachment needs.

If, after being hurt, you quietly soothed yourself rather than seeking support you are more likely to have an avoidant attachment style. If you were upset and could only be calmed in the arms of a parent, grandparent or someone you trust, you are more likely to have an anxious attachment style. If you used a combination of seeking out help as you needed and also calmed yourself, it is more likely that you are securely attached.

Life is richer than one childhood accident, of course. Many other events have shaped your life. Even so, this memory is a fairly accurate guide to your attachment needs.

If you need to, read over this chapter again and ask yourself, 'What are my attachment needs? Am I basically secure, or avoidant or anxious?' Knowing the answer to this will help you as we move through the CPR strategies.

ASSESS THE PULSE OF YOUR RELATIONSHIP

Let's just draw a breath for a moment and see where you are now. Is your relationship:

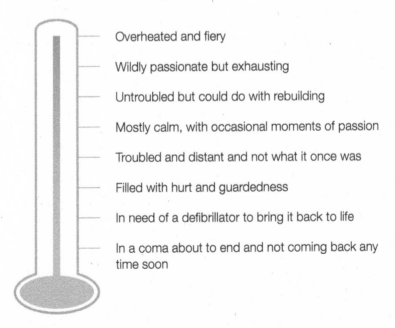

Overheated and fiery

Wildly passionate but exhausting

Untroubled but could do with rebuilding

Mostly calm, with occasional moments of passion

Troubled and distant and not what it once was

Filled with hurt and guardedness

In need of a defibrillator to bring it back to life

In a coma about to end and not coming back any time soon

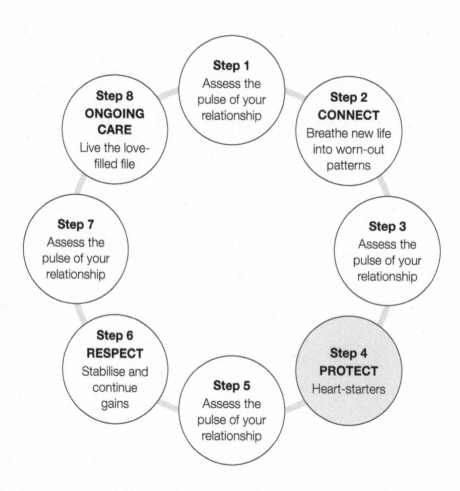

CPR model: Connect, protect and respect

PROTECT
HEART-STARTERS FOR A BETTER RELATIONSHIP AND A BETTER WAY OF BEING

We are only as healthy as our relationships. Our relationships are where we belong and seek solace and a sense of haven from life; they are where we play and love and laugh; they are the source of our wounds and the basis of our worries; they can nourish our soul or crush our spirit; they teach us about other people; and, importantly, they teach us about ourselves. Our relationships can embolden and expand our lives or trap us in a dark prison; they can expand our sense of who we are or diminish us to the point where we become desiccated versions of ourselves. To a large extent, our relationships define who we are.

This chapter on protection is about changing the nature of relationships. To protect is to take care of the other person and yourself. It is moving from being a reactor to being a creator.

By creating a relationship you become vulnerable. In the CPR approach to relationships a decisive factor is the contribution each person makes to the relationship. Love flows in the direction of giving. To live better, give better.

To live better, give better.

Love is life's greatest prize — the love and commitment of that special person. It is perhaps the greatest and most precious prize that any of us can aspire to in this life. It is a prize of far greater worth and far more satisfying than any material prize or social distinction or fame.

So guard this prize carefully. Protect it, care for it, allow it to grow, nourish it and nurture it. It is humanity's greatest gift.

Imagine for a moment that you are in a relationship with someone you care for or love deeply and you have made a mistake. You make a sincere apology. What do you hope the other person will do?

- Return the 'favour'?
- Keep bringing up the mistake and making you feel bad about it?
- Accept that you have made a mistake and maybe feel hurt by it, but slowly forgive you and move on?

In the first two responses, the relationship moves to a transactional basis. There is a trade-off and a ledger sheet. If you stick to a practice of 'if you hurt me, I'll hurt you' the relationship will go into resuscitation mode and the chances of recovery will become slim.

The people you are in relationships with, by and large, are the people you chose to be in relationships with. It wasn't a choice you made flippantly, lightly or even accidentally. You have an obligation to protect the choice you made as much as you can.

This means the way we deal with the mistakes and how we act to protect our relationships are crucial. This chapter focuses on the contribution you make to your relationships.

By understanding your own contribution, you are in a more powerful position to create positive relationships.

One of the great investments of life is the time you put into becoming a better conversationalist.

Changing your relationship language

The words that we speak form our conversations and our conversations are the glue that links us in relationships. In some ways conversations are like songs sung between people: when they are in harmony the outcome is beautiful; when they are discordant they sound fractious and dreadful.

One of the great investments of life is the time you put into becoming a better conversationalist. Even shy, introverted people can develop their conversational skills.

As in many areas of life, we form general patterns in the way we respond to hearing good news:[6]

- **Amplifying** positive emotions. You say something good about your life and amplifiers say, 'That's great to hear' and ask more about it.

- **Stalling** the conversation with little or no emotional involvement. You tell someone in this mode something good about your life and they stall by saying something like, 'I suppose that's good' or 'That's nice for you.' Typically this shuts down the sharing of positive information and the conversation turns to other topics.

- **Deflating** reduces the good news by pointing out problems. You tell someone in this mode some good news and they deflate by pointing out potential pitfalls or issues. For example, you might tell them that you have a new job and will move to a great location and they will ask whether you can afford it. What about your friends? Is the place as good as it seems? This is often expressed as concern but acts as a needle of cynicism to your balloon of hopefulness and happiness.

- **Stealing** the limelight by changing the subject. Usually these people feel they have more important news, issues and ideas than yours.

Let's use an example – someone comes home and says, 'I've been given a promotion.' As we learn our conversation style when we are children, think about how the family you grew up in would have responded to that statement.

	Constructive	Destructive
Active	*Amplifying* 'That's great, well done! You've worked hard and you deserve it.'	*Deflating* 'Now you'll have to spend even more time at work.'
Passive	*Stalling* 'That's nice.'	*Stealing* 'Oh, is that what happened to you today? Wait till you hear what happened to me ...'

Time to become your own language coach

Even if you are not by nature an effusive person, practising conversational skills pays off, big time! Think about the most important relationship in your life. How much time do you spend amplifying, deflating, stalling or stealing? How do you respond to good news from other people? How do you respond to bad news?

Changing your relationships to connect, protect and respect more will require you to initiate the change and lead the way. Take on this project for yourself: be someone who contributes to conversations and amplifies positivity as much as possible. Do this is for all the conversations you have for several weeks. Notice but don't comment when other people deflate, stall or steal through their conversations. Continue to amplify and provide contributions even in conversations where other people are not contributing in the same way.

Know how relationships work

There are two ways in which most people understand relationships and ruin them in the process.

Tennis court

Many people see their relationships as if they were on a tennis court and their responsibilities only cover their side of the net. The net is the dividing line. Whatever is on their side of the net they can take responsibility for and fix. Whatever is on the other side of the net is the other person's doing and is their responsibility to fix.

Sounds reasonable so far, doesn't it? Each person is responsible for their own actions. That sounds fair, doesn't it? Well, no: there is a glitch in this neat and popular way of viewing relationships. It is almost as if there are four rules:

- Rule No. 1. My side of the net is perfect.
- Rule No. 2. Any problems that occur are due to issues on the other person's side of the net.

- Rule No. 3. When a problem occurs, remember Rule No. 1.
- Rule No. 4. If a problem needs fixing, remember Rule No. 2.

There is a human tendency to see our actions as good and blameless and, when problems occur, the other person's actions as self-serving and sneaky. We can then apportion blame and despair: 'If only he was more loving.' 'If only she would be true to me.' 'If only he would pay me more attention.' 'If only she would give me some space.' 'If only he could stop eyeing off other women.' And on and on it goes.

While we may not be able to alter other people's actions, to be powerful in relationships we need to try. In order to do so we need to adopt a view of relationships that may seem unfair and unreasonable – act as if we are responsible for the entire tennis court, not just our side of the net. Take on caring for our side of the net, the other side, the fence, the surroundings, the whole box and dice. In other words, assume responsibility for *everything* that happens in a relationship. This means you will be asking yourself questions like: 'How do I create that in our relationship? How do I act differently to create a different outcome? What can I do in the future to improve how we get along?'

Now obviously this approach has its exceptions. I am not suggesting you become a victim and stay in a violent or abusive relationship. What I am saying is that for most of your relationships with others in which direct abuse or violence is not occurring, act as if you are the cause, the creator and at times the solver of anything that happens within that relationship.

As delusional as this might sound, it places you in a powerful position to alter and improve your life and the relationships you have with others.

Tit-for-tat

Tit-for-tat is the basis of many relationships. Essentially this means that if you treat me well, I'll treat you well, but if you treat me badly, I'll treat you badly in return. This behaviour is the cause of much misery in people's lives.

Tit-for-tat seems okay at first: it starts out nice and cooperative; it means you get along with people; it is not passive, so if you do something nasty to me, I will do or say something nasty back to you.

So far it sounds fair and reasonable – but trouble awaits.

Let's use an example. Imagine that you and I work together. We are not close colleagues but we have a good working relationship and we have a ritual: every morning I come in and say, 'Good morning', then you say, 'Good morning, Andrew', and we get on with the business of the day.

Then one morning I come in and say, 'Good morning', and you don't reply. If I were following tit-for-tat principles I might think, 'How insulting! I've been snubbed by you; I'm not going to have that! I am never going to say good morning to you again.'

There are several problems with this tit-for-tat response. First, the relationship is being led by the person who 'appears' to have behaved the most shabbily. If this keeps up, the nasty people rule the world. Is that what we want?

Second, I have no idea why you didn't greet me that morning. Something upsetting happening at home? Ear infection? Distracted and worried? Who knows! So I could give you the benefit of the doubt and continue to greet you in the morning.

A third possible way of handling this is to be true to yourself. Ask yourself what you stand for as a friend/partner/colleague/family member and act in accordance with those beliefs or values. If asked, I would say I want to be a kind and helpful person so, holding to the truth of who I am, I would continue to say good morning.

This brings us to the next stage of understanding relationships so we can lead them in positive directions.

CPR emotional regulation in relationships

The most helpful way of seeing relationships is that we are all in the business of soothing ourselves and our partners, colleagues, friends and family. Caring for each other maintains the oxygen supply in all our relationships.

In our lives there is a balance between the demands and challenges we face and the skills and resources we have to deal with them. When we have enough resources (time, love, money, support) and skills to manage the demands we face, we are fine. If we have more demands than we can cope with, we become stressed and agitated. It's not ideal, either, if we have lots of skills and too few demands: we become stressed and bored and even give up.

There are three main relationship states:

1. Resilient

A successful relationship of any kind – familial, friendship, collegial, teacher–student and romantic – occurs in an optimal zone. There is a balance between the challenges or problems faced and the skills available to meet them.

2. Anxious

When the challenges or problems exceed our skills we become anxious, agitated, scratchy, thoughtless and attacking. We are ruled by fear and stress, and we respond in ways that will reduce our fearful feelings, but not always in the most constructive manner.

3. Avoidant

When our skills exceed the challenges we become bored, disinterested and listless. If we add stress to this mix we give up, can't be bothered and think, 'What's the point?'

We can easily see agitation as a sign of stress but it is important to learn that avoidance and absenteeism are also expressions of stress. In both cases, people are trying to get back to being in the resilient zone.

When we are out of the resilient zone we know it: we don't feel right. In successful relationships we start to see these signals in ourselves and learn how to get back to the resilient zone as quickly as possible. Then we learn what signs show us that our partners are either anxious or avoidant and work out ways to help them get back into the resilient zone too.

In successful relationships you will know more about how to get your partner back into the resilient zone than they do, helping to build a secure relationship. And when you build a secure relationship, everyone wins.

People are almost always trying to do the best they can to get back into the resilient zone. We are all healthier and happier in the resilient zone than out of it.

The problem is, the ways many of us have learned to do this don't work. Even worse, some of the strategies *seem* to work but don't work for very long. Ineffective methods include arguing, yelling, drinking alcohol, working too hard, flirting with others and checking social media for long periods of time.

The key to successful relationships

You may know this from your own life. If your partner comes home feeling overwhelmed, edgy or stressed, you may know how to soothe them back into the resilient zone. If you are wise, you might say, 'Take it easy/have a seat on the couch/have a drink/do you want to talk about it/don't worry, I'll fix dinner.'

Alternatively, there might be times when your partner has been kicking around the house, a bit bored, a bit listless and a bit restless. Hopefully you have the wherewithal to say, 'Let's

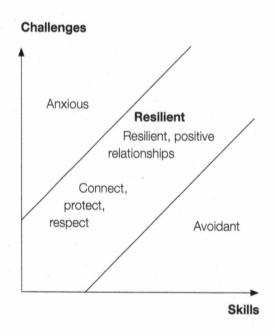

go out/catch a movie/go for a walk/visit friends/have a picnic.' By doing this you can bring them back into the resilient zone.

Try to remember a time when you noticed your partner was upset. What helpful things did you do to get them back into the resilient zone? When we are in the resilient zone we can learn, be present and mindful, and make good decisions about our lives and relationships. The more time we spend in the zone the more positive and creative we are and the more effectively our immune systems function, so we also tend to live longer.[7]

When we are anxious and agitated we are too wired, frazzled and reactive. When we are avoidant, we are not involved. We are overly passive, sullen, sad, dejected, defeated, tired, or just too defensive to be with people.

The more time all of us spend in the resilient zone, the happier we are. And the more time our relationships spend in this zone the more satisfying they are.

There are skills that we can learn to help ourselves return to the resilient zone. There are skills that we can learn to use to help others to be in the zone most of the time. While it may take some time to learn exactly how to soothe agitation and absenteeism in yourself and others, it is without doubt a gift that keeps on giving.

If we feel better in the resilient zone than out of it, why don't people just stay in it?

Being in relationships with others involves making ourselves vulnerable. Vulnerability can topple easily into anxiety and fear, and all of us have ways of protecting ourselves when we feel scared. These are sometimes referred to as defence mechanisms that we have used from childhood to cope with fears and problems we can't solve. They are not conscious and they do not solve the problem, but they do ease fear.

Defence mechanisms	
Agitated	**Absent**
Projection – Blame someone else, see your own faults in others	**Denial** – 'It wasn't me, or it didn't happen'
Sublimation – 'I'll work harder, be better'	**Turning against the self** – 'It's my fault'
Rationalisation – 'I didn't want it anyway'	**Regression** – Acting in childlike ways
Intellectualisation – Debating issues at length	**Displacement** – Relieving hurts through distractions such as gambling, drinking, time spent on computers or devices
Reaction formation – Overcompensating (e.g. being mean to someone we like)	**Fantasy** – Thinking about ex-partners, switching off, daydreaming, porn

How stress affects us

What moves us from the resilient zone to either being agitated or absent is stress.[8]

Stress has the capacity to drive us all crazy, but it is also the reason we are all here. Let's explain.

FREEZE

Our ancestors had a problem. Their problem was how to survive – and of course if they hadn't survived, we wouldn't be here. Our ancestors' big idea was that in the face of a threat like a sabre-toothed tiger, they should lie down and pretend to be dead. This was a rabbit-in-the-headlights strategy, and not much of a safety policy. It was based on the idea that most predators would either be too stupid or too busy to come over and have a sniff and a bite.

So in the face of threat they stopped, stayed very still and 'froze'. We often think about 'freeze' as a very primitive response to stress but we have all done it. If you have ever been shocked speechless, you know 'freeze'. If you have ever opened up a test or exam paper and had your memories melt away, you know 'freeze'.

It is the same response that puts us into the lower part of the diagram on p. 68. We give up, surrender, remove ourselves, become absent, disengage and become unmotivated.

The idea of freezing in the face of threat wasn't terribly successful. Not all predators were that busy and they weren't always that stupid, either. To increase their chances of survival, our ancestors therefore developed a better response.

FIGHT/FLIGHT

Our ancestors developed a great innovation you probably know as the fight/flight response. Rather than lying down and pretending to be dead, they revved up their systems. Their amygdalae, the threat-detecting parts of their brains, engineered the release of the stress hormone cortisol. Their amygdalae also signalled to their adrenal glands on the top of their kidneys to release adrenaline. Suddenly they were pumped and ready for action. Their blood supply shifted away from their internal organs to their muscles, preparing them to either run away or fight it out. As Robert Sapolsky, Professor of Neurological Sciences at Stanford University, puts it, this part of the stress response is good for moments when either it's over or you're over.[9]

The fight/flight response puts us into the anxious, upper part of the diagram on p. 68. We become antsy, cranky, grumpy, wary, snarky, argumentative and generally not our usual wonderful selves.

The big problem was that the bodies of some of our ancestors couldn't tell the difference between a sabre-toothed tiger situation and solving a tricky relationship issue. So some of them developed stress-related illnesses and some of them did not survive. This wasn't good because if they didn't survive we weren't going to be here. So our ancestors developed a third way of managing stress.

CONNECT, PROTECT, RESPECT

This third way is togetherness with other people. When we do things in harmony, in synchrony, we calm one another. This is why we often find catching up with friends, being with people we love, singing together, dancing together or talking together to be so soul enriching. We feel connected, protected and respected.

This is when we, and the people we are with, are in the resilient zone. Learning to bring yourself out of freeze or fight/flight and back into the resilient zone is one of the best ways you can create a great life and a great relationship.

There are times for all of us when we topple out of the zone and into freeze or flight/fight mode. There are times when we become absent or agitated. Our aim is to spend as much time in the resilient zone as we possibly can. Then we can have our relationships in this zone for most of the time.

Our aim is to also make the resilient zone as broad as possible. You might have met people for whom if one tiny thing goes wrong, it is a disaster. Other people sail through life reasonably unruffled. The reason they can do this is because they know how to broaden their resilient zone most of the time, and when they are agitated or absent they get themselves back into this zone relatively quickly and easily.

The more time you spend in the resilient zone, the more trust you can build. The more trust there is, the more secure you feel. Feeling secure means you can broaden your resilient zone.

What successful relationships have in common

All successful relationships – romantic, in workplaces, sports teams, leadership teams, friendships, families – occur in the resilient zone. It is here that we can be productive, happy, engaged and creative. Humans have never functioned well for any length of time when they feel disconnected, unsafe and disrespected.

De-agitators

To calm ourselves and other people, we need routines and systems. These are tested over time with the people around us. Some strategies that work to bring people from agitation and back to the resilient zone are:*

Sleep

Reading a book

Going online

Eating

Resting

Back rubs

Exercise

Music

A bath

Changing out of work clothes

A snack

Drinking water

Planning

Pets

Walking

Singing

Dancing

Completing a project

Massage

Being left alone (for some)

Conversations and being listened to (for some; others want to be left alone)

Things that generally *do not* work include: arguing, yelling, having mistakes pointed out, alcohol, drugs, conflict, deadlines, multiple demands, sex, being left alone (for some, as they can feel agitated and abandoned), and conversations and being listened to (for some; others want to talk).

* Calming agitation is more difficult with anxiously attached people, as they can take longer to be sure you are there for them. Some will even feel unworthy of your attempts to help and calm them.

How to soothe agitation

You come home from work edgy and fractious. Hopefully someone has the wisdom to say something like, 'Would you like a cup of tea? Put your feet up, it looks like you've had a tough day.'

Learn to welcome people into your care. In fact, it is useful to presume that most people you meet have been in a torrid battle and need to be with you for a bit before they can feel safe and calm. This is especially true when your partner comes home from work. Greet them warmly and act as if they have come to you from a fairly difficult situation.

How to soothe absenteeism

You are lying around at home feeling shattered after a hard week at work. Hopefully someone says something like, 'How about resting up for a bit, then let's go to the beach for a swim.' They gently help you to move from being absent to being present.

When you are agitated and your partner is absent

Start by being self-soothing. Calm yourself first so that you are then able to express your concerns or feelings calmly and constructively. Remind yourself that your partner does not have the same brain as you, so won't know what's happening in your head. Mind-reading is notoriously unreliable!

De-escalate your own thinking. Take some time to let go of brooding thoughts and breathe. You might need to hit the pause button. You may decide that this situation needs to be dealt with later when you have calmed down.

If your concerns are still around the next day, raise them when you both have the time and space to talk about them in a collaborative manner – avoid blaming, criticising and contempt.

When you are absent and your partner is agitated

Here you are, pleasantly minding your own business and they begin rattling the pans in the background, stomping through the house or rummaging through the drawers. You might be quietly flicking through social media sites minding your own business while they keep interrupting and wanting to talk. They may be tossing and turning in bed while you are sleeping. They may be brooding over a recent upset while you are oblivious to the whole thing.

The time-honoured questions 'Is something the matter?', 'Are you upset?' and 'What's wrong?' are not advisable.

If the reply is 'nothing', something is definitely up. Work on the premise that they have an upset, so there is a problem that needs solving. 'How can I help' may also be a better question, or simply be more present with them.

Pay attention. Don't ignore their attempts to connect – if you do they will become even more agitated. Your partner's antennae for connection is twitching and needs soothing. Pay attention and look for ways to provide comfort.

Look for ways to connect. As Gary Chapman (1995) mentions in his wonderful book *The Five Love Languages*, some people see different gestures as signs of love – time, gifts, acts of service, touch, words of affirmation such as being told 'I love you'. It might be washing the dishes or cleaning up. It might be listening attentively to the latest family news. It might be being there and being prepared to listen to how their day has been.

Moving from absent to present

Generally, shifting from being absent to being present requires either more patience or more spontaneity. Sometimes giving people the opportunity to become present at their own rate works better than rushing them.

Some strategies that often work include:

- being hugged
- being made a drink
- being kissed
- being listened to
- being looked after
- being given time and space to recover
- asking, 'Do you need some time for yourself?', or 'Is there anything I can get you?' or 'Let me know if you would like to talk about things later.'

Some strategies that *do not* work include: being blamed, making accusations, criticising, rushing and trying to joke people out of their mood.

Being heard and being acknowledged or validated allows us to lower our defences and move towards connecting. This can take longer for avoidantly attached people.

The big five

The five values that underpin successful relationships are, in order:

1. trust

2. forgiveness

3. integrity

4. hope

5. compassion.[10]

TRUST

Trust is the sense that we can rely on and depend upon one another. More relationships are torn apart by broken trust than by boredom, incompatibility or 'falling out of love'. Trust is the basis of all successful relationships.[11]

To enter into a relationship requires a degree of trust: we make ourselves vulnerable to the other and in doing so trust that they will care for us. All of us are wired to trust. In fact, we are so trusting that we do it with even thinking about it. If you have ever travelled on a plane or in a train, or eaten in a restaurant, you have trusted someone you've never met.

Trust is also the reason we are all here. Our ancestors' ability to trust others, form tribes, and collaborate and work together enhanced their survival prospects.[12]

Of course, we are wary at times when we feel our trust may have been misplaced or taken advantage of. We often evaluate the potential costs of misplaced trust over the benefits of trusting people. This is not always our best calculation or in our best interests. We can be wary and distant when there is no reason to be.

This may also be why we reserve our harshest criticisms for those we have trusted if they let us down. This may also be why the loss of love hits us so hard.

The pathway to trust begins with tentative steps. To shift from wariness to trust is an act of courage. We cannot live alone, nor can we love alone. We have no choice about that. What we do have is a choice about the quality of that loving relationship.

FORGIVENESS

There are two great tests of trust:

- to trust someone in the first place
- to trust someone after something has gone wrong.

We are all human and we all make mistakes. In every relationship there are slip-ups, mistakes and hurtful misunderstandings. How we manage these moments defines the relationship. A decision-making tree for forgiveness is outlined on the next page.

DEALING WITH MISTAKES

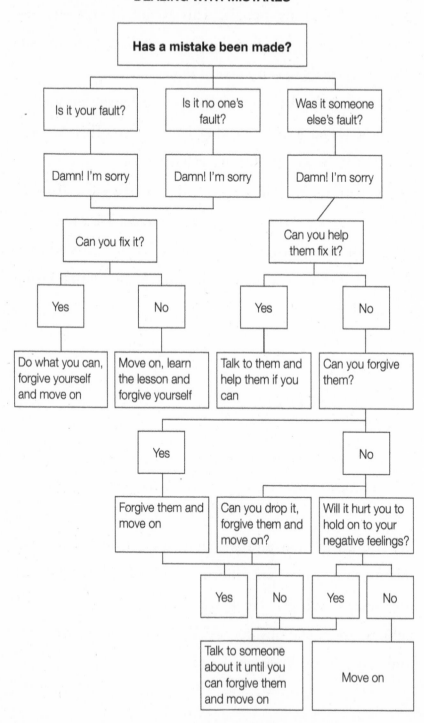

Love and romance are often portrayed so rosily in our culture that the reality of a flesh-and-blood relationship may be disappointing by comparison. Ultimately we need to accept our partners and our relationships as they are.

When we are hurt or harmed, there is a choice to either retaliate or repair. If we retaliate the relationship will be on a downward spiral and heading for the emergency room. The pathway of repair and healing is the path of forgiveness.

Forgiveness is not weakness. It is not forgetting. It is not even acceptance. It is acknowledgement of what has happened and making the choice to move on.

As my colleague John Hendry says, to understand the word 'forgive', reverse the two syllables, 'give-for'. When we forgive, we give-for the relationship and we give-for ourselves.

We have all had to forgive someone in our lives. We have all been let down or disappointed by someone, yet stayed in a relationship or friendship with them. If we were unable to forgive we would be lonely.

Similarly, we have all been forgiven. Anyone who has ever had parents has been forgiven. Anyone who still has some friends has also been forgiven.

Forgiveness is an act of self-compassion. Forgiveness allows us not to be defined by the person who has harmed us. It is a gift to others but it is also a gift to ourselves.

Of course, it can take some time before we feel strong enough to give. It is always important that our voice, our pain and our story are heard and understood. This begins the process of healing and repair.

It is important to take time to overcome the hurt, the shame, the damage and the loss. As painful as this can feel sometimes, forgiveness is our only way forward. It frees us to move beyond disappointment and resume our lives.

Even if the other person does not see that they have caused hurt or pain and even if they show no sign of remorse, it is still worth freeing ourselves through forgiveness.

Forgiveness is a way of saying, 'Although I have been hurt I need to move on. I need to give to myself and to the person or people who have hurt me so we can all move beyond this. I can restore dignity for myself.'

The pain can only be transformed when we have healed enough to forgive and have forgiven. Forgiveness allows a gathering together of the parts of us that have not been damaged or hurt to gain strength and heal the parts that have been hurt. We become whole again.

INTEGRITY

Integrity is being who we say we are and doing what we say we will do. It is about being authentic. Establishing trust builds relationships; forgiving mistakes cements relationships; acting with integrity builds new ways of relating.

We seek out integrity in ourselves and in other people. We want ideas, people and actions on which we can meaningfully rely. We want to relate to people we can believe in.

We also want to act with integrity and often feel ashamed when our actions don't match our words or ideals. The situations in which we lose integrity are often the situations that haunt us later on, with regrets.

When integrity is lost, trust is broken. It is replaced by suspicion, wariness and anxiety. These are the signs of fear. There are times in all our lives when fear is an ally. It can save our lives. When fear dominates in a relationship, however, it saps trust and confidence.

Guarded, distant or distrustful relationships bring us no joy or nourishment. These are relationships that either need to be changed or left.

HOPE

Hope protects us against despair and depression. It is a vital element in a happy life and an essential ingredient in healing. Hope is the belief that together we can create a better future. When there is hope, each person gives freely to strengthen the relationship, enabling the other to do so as well. Hope gives us confidence in the ongoing nature of the relationship and strengthens our level of contribution.

COMPASSION

Compassion involves understanding people's feelings and situations and doing something to care for them. Compassion is being able to recognise when people are either agitated or absent, and being prepared to take constructive action with the necessary steps to help them to get back into the resilient zone. Compassion is the foundation of connecting, protecting and respecting.

Compassion is the foundation of
connecting, protecting and respecting.

Love is fuelled by compassion. It is the capacity to value others as well as ourselves. Relationships are constructed on the contribution we can make to our partners, not on what advantage we can gain. To be filled with compassion is to look beyond ourselves, to enjoy shared possibilities and to discover what creates pain and try to remedy it.

Compassion is contagious. There is a ripple effect in all of our lives: quality relationships create more quality relationships. This ripple effect is powerful. Hopefulness replaces helplessness. Trust replaces fear. Connection is more prominent than judgement. Caring overrides divisions. Forgiveness and compassion allow us to heal, grow and flourish.

Bringing together trust, forgiveness, integrity, hope and compassion increases our capacity to create positive changes in our world. These positive changes in turn unlock those capacities in the people around us. When this is truly present in us it has the same effect on our relationships that springtime has on daffodils.

How to apologise

Even when we have the big five values – trust, forgiveness, integrity, hope and compassion – in place most of the time, things still can go awfully wrong. There are times when all of us should sincerely apologise.

It takes a lot to admit you did something wrong. Don't be afraid to admit that you messed up. It happens to all of us. Someone who can swallow their pride and admit they're in the wrong is a great contributor to a relationship.

A genuine apology includes the pronoun 'I' and does not include the word 'but'. You may have received an insincere apology in your life. Someone may have said, 'Oh I'm so sorry', then listed a series of reasons why they did what they did. This usually sounds more like excuses. An authentic apology is something like, 'I really didn't mean to hurt your feelings. I am sorry.'

It will take time for some people to accept an apology. They need this time. Just because we are ready to apologise and try to make amends, it doesn't mean that the other person is also ready. Even if this feels unfair, we need to respect their point of view.

Follow up a few days later either in person or with a note saying something like, 'I really want to apologise for what happened and to ask you what I can do to fix the situation. What I did was wrong and I don't want it to end or harm a great relationship.'

Pulse report

The CPR approach encourages us to think about ways we can make a more positive contribution to our relationships. It involves learning to calm ourselves and our partners. It is about building and maintaining the values that positive relationships possess: trust, forgiveness, integrity, hope and compassion. It is also about accepting that we and everyone we relate to are human. We make mistakes. They will make mistakes. CPR is about apologising for mistakes and repairing moments where things have gone wrong. By doing this we build respect.

ASSESS THE PULSE OF YOUR RELATIONSHIP

Okay, it's time to get out the thermometer again and assess your relationship. Let's do a quick review first. We've thought about:

- how language affects relationships and tried to change our own language to be more positively amplifying
- why tennis-court behaviour patterns and tit-for-tat thinking destroy relationships
- how all of us operate best when the challenges we face and the skills we have are in balance
- how when we are not in the resilient zone we become either anxious and agitated or absent

- how we can learn the signs in ourselves when we are out of the resilient zone and learn how to get back into it
- how we can see the signs in other people when they are out of the resilient zone and learn ways to help them get back into the zone
- the five values that underpin successful relationships: trust, forgiveness, integrity, hope and compassion.

Now grab your thermometer – it's time to measure where you're at. Which best describes your relationship?

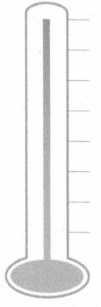

We spend most of our time in the resilient zone

We forgive each other

Trust, forgiveness, integrity, hope and compassion are present

We spend a fair degree of time in the agitated zone

We spend a fair degree of time in the absent zone

We spend lots of time in both the agitated and absent zones and can't seem to get out of them

We need a defibrillator to resuscitate our relationship

Our relationship is in a coma, about to end and not coming back anytime soon

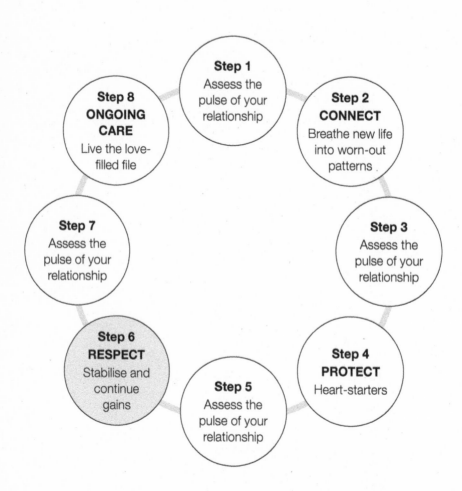

CPR model: Connect, protect and respect

RESPECT
STABILISE AND CONTINUE GAINS

'Tread softly because you tread on my dreams.'

W.B. Yeats

Care, maintenance and rebuilding

So far we have covered the type of partner you are, your attachment style, how to shift the language in your relationship and how to keep your relationship in the resilient zone. Now we need to talk about what has happened to the relationship. We need to do this to settle any residual resentments and also to make sure whatever happened doesn't happen again. To do this, let's give you another way to think about your relationship, called 'the eclipse model of relationships'.

Early on it was you two and the world. Your world wasn't perfect but it was fun, loving and pretty good.

'Us'   Problems

There were some problems – not because the relationship inherently had problems but because life always presents us with challenges. Look around at the bills to pay, dishes to wash, mouths to feed and mess to clean up …

Gradually, those problems infiltrated your relationship. Tensions grew. Feelings were hurt. People felt less loved and less respected. An overlap appeared and you were no longer people who *had* problems – one or both of you *became* the problem.

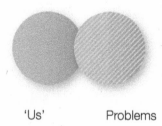

'Us'   Problems

In some cases, this caused a split in the relationship. A shift from 'us' to 'you' and 'me'.

You

Problems

Me

Problems

This was when blame, sniping, resentments and taking cheap shots crept into your relationship. Thoughts like the following found their way into your lives:

- 'Why am I always the one who cleans up?'
- 'We never seem to do what I want to do.'
- 'I wish you would help more.'
- 'If I didn't initiate sex we would never have sex.'
- 'If you didn't spend so much money doing what you want, I wouldn't have to work so much.'

Quite possibly these thoughts occurred to both of you. In an unguarded, loose-lipped moment, these private grumbling, rumbling thoughts showed themselves and disappointments became accusations. Hurt was expressed as anger. Most likely the true weapons of mass destruction, shame and blame, were used.

It makes sense to feel so hurt and disappointed. After all, we hold the highest hopes for the people we love. We want the best for them and we also want them to want the best for us.

At this stage the relationship usually moves from loving cooperation to transactional counting. Little issues loom as big battles:

- 'I fed the cat last time.'
- 'Have you forgotten when I got home early and took the kids to the park?'
- 'You slept in last weekend while I did the shopping.'
- 'Who do you think earns the money to pay for all of this?'
- 'Well, what do you think I've been doing all day – having a bath?'

Transactional squabbling is always a sign that a relationship is in trouble. This often involves counting how many times who did what most recently. Some people settle for this and bunker down for the rest of their lives sniping at each other and feeling that their own lives have been stunted by the person they have chosen to be with. Their relationships resemble prisons.

Even if things have not become so severe in your own relationship, the problems can loom so powerfully you no longer really see the other person or the relationship. You are both eclipsed by the problems.

You   Problems

Me   Problems

This is when the CPR process can start to revolutionise the relationship. By patiently implementing the steps in this book you will begin to experience the following developmental stages.

Connecting

Initially, reconnecting links you both. The problems are still powerful influences but relearning your and your partner's styles of attachment, the type of lover they are and what to do when they are either agitated or absent helps you to see them again as the person they are.

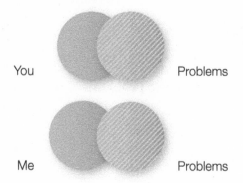

As problems start to dominate less, your view of each other clears and intimacy is reborn, albeit tentatively. Attachment needs are discussed and hopefully met. Trust begins with tiny steps but builds. If mistakes are forgiven, we help one another to act with integrity.

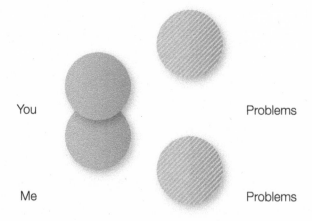

Slowly and steadily, a new category of 'us' returns from the separate world of 'you' and 'me'. Problems that obscured who you both are and what you could be are still problems but they can be tackled together. They are not confused with who you are as people. You are healing and growing stronger in your relationship. It is still early days but the signs are looking positive. Hope re-emerges.

Then something shocking almost always happens. An issue rises, an old wound becomes sensitive or a dispute flares up. The feeling that often accompanies this is despair. Just when we were getting somewhere!

You   Problems

Me   Problems

This collapse occurs because of the power of the past. Fears rise up. Intimacy is a risk. We feel vulnerable and anxious.

We all carry within us wounds from previous relationships. We may not even be conscious of them but they sit inside us waiting for expression. These are the times when we felt let down, misunderstood, disappointed, betrayed or sad. These may not be things our current partner has anything to do with.

Your parents weren't perfect. Your siblings weren't perfect. Your past romantic partners certainly weren't perfect. All of these people have, mostly without meaning to, left a trail of sensitivities within you.

These sensitivities and wounds cause you to overreact to some issues. We can all take some messages hurtfully and connect them to unrelated events. A few examples are:

- 'When you don't clean up, I feel you don't love me.'
- 'Not picking up after yourself is disrespectful.'
- 'If you truly loved me you would know what I am feeling.'
- 'When you are tired I feel boring and uninteresting.'

There are times for all of us when we should examine our thinking and assumptions with a wary eye. Assuming that our own point of view is always right and beyond our own doubt and questioning is dangerous territory.

It is a day of enlightenment for all of us when we finally look inside our heads and ask ourselves, 'Who is making this stuff up?' The realisation that not all of our thoughts are equally sane, that some ideas should be done away with, is a useful insight.

Learning to be curious about our own feelings and thoughts, and being prepared to question their validity, helps us to be more considerate of other people's perspectives. These are the moments that will test you and test your relationship. You can either move into retaliatory mode and consolidate all the fears or use forgiveness.

You

Us

Me

Problems

Problems

It will take enormous strength of mind to resist the pull of the past and not tumble back into the world of shame and blame, of hurt and retaliation. To achieve this you need to think carefully about what sort of relationship you want to have and you will also need skills you may not previously have had to guide yourself and your partner to a revolutionary CPR way of relating.

As you make progress in your relationship you need to plan to ensure the changes continue. The weekly planner on the next page will help you decide your key actions. These are the contributions you can make to a new relationship.

Set aside some time each week to decide the priorities for your relationship. Generally I recommend people repeat this plan for at least six weeks. Some of my clients, however, find this so helpful they keep using it for much longer.

Each week, write down one thing in each quadrant you think you should do that will have a positive impact on your relationship.

CPR RELATIONSHIP WEEKLY PLANNER

What should I do more of?	What should I do less of?
What should I start doing?	What should I stop doing?

The sign that I will use this week as an indicator of success is:

Write down one helpful thing you will do more of, one unhelpful thing you will do less of, one constructive thing you will start doing and one destructive thing you will stop doing. Then, write down what your personal sign of success will be. Make it a small sign or even just a slight indicator. Relationship patterns take time to build up and they also take time to dissolve.

Except when people are at risk of harm, it is always best to go slow. There will be gains as well as setbacks as you progress through the next few weeks.

In a world that drives people apart and makes them 'crazy-busy', being a partner who pauses and thinks about the most important thing they could do in the next week is a major advantage.

Arguing fairly and respectfully

We all come ill-prepared for the sensitivities of arguing in romantic relationships. Before you became romantically involved, almost all of your arguments with similar-aged people were with some peers who turned out not to be your friends, or with your siblings. In both cases there is an intensity and sometimes a ferocity to those arguments that doesn't work well in the tender world of romantic relationships.

Knowing how to win an argument and knowing how to argue well are two entirely different things. One is usually a winner-takes-all approach, while arguing well resolves the issue and restores the relationship. Arguments happen. It's the way they happen that really matters.

Arguments happen. It's the way they happen that really matters.

Major arguments are the proverbial icebergs: there are the visible issues (the dishes being done, the house being tidy, who takes charge of the remote control, who picks up the kids, who arranges social outings or catch-ups) and the out-of-sight matters of the heart. To grow through conflict we need to focus on the out-of-sight matters of the heart just as much as the issue at hand.

Some conflict is normal in relationships. Done well, arguing and differences of approach can lead to better ways of relating. Done badly, arguing leads to the issue bubbling away unresolved, simmering until it erupts again.

The re-emergence of the issue catches everyone off guard. The person who has been ruminating over the problem may feel hurt, unheard and uncared for. The conflict usually simmers away and then, at a later time, escapes the leash in an unguarded moment.

This surprises the person who thought the issue was resolved. There is a 'here-we-go-again' moment that feels disheartening. The repetitive, cyclic nature of many of these types of arguments can grind the life out of relationships.

This means we need to learn to look for what might be lurking out of sight and the way to do this is to have the intention of connect, protect and respect.

The CPR way of arguing

When people argue with you they are trying to help you find a better way of doing things. (They may not always be doing this well, of course!) And there's no point having an argument about who is washing the dishes if, as soon as that is solved, you are arguing about what to watch on television.

Earlier in this book we talked about two ways people often sabotage their relationship: by using tit-for-tat or treating their relationship like a tennis court, with all of the mistakes being made on the other side of the net. The CPR way of arguing is that if you have a problem, then we have a problem, and if I have a problem, then I would like us to try to solve it together.

CONNECT

We all need to have a voice in the decisions that affect our lives. When we feel we don't have a voice, we raise our voice.

We have a choice in life as well as in arguments: are we going to prove we are right or are we going to aim for happiness? Arguments, even those about straightforward issues, are complicated. In a speeded-up world we overly simplify things rather than deal with complexities. It is so easy to demonise the other person, make it their fault, see ourselves as perfect or blameless and in need of a well-deserved apology. This is an area where you can win the battle but certainly not the war.

In any conflict our first step is to try to understand the person who does not understand us. This means asking the person you have some conflict with to tell you their way of viewing things.

Listen.

Don't interject. Don't defend. Don't deny the issue. Definitely don't try to use humour to deflect the issue.

Listen attentively. If you can, listen in two ways – once for the issue or problem being described, a second way for the emotion underlying the complaint.

This means managing your primitive brain. Your primitive brain wants to protect you. It feels offended, misunderstood and falsely accused on your behalf. It wants to defend you vigorously or storm off in a huff.

Ideally in an argument you state your point once and then wait to hear the other person's point of view. If you find yourself repeating or elaborating the same point or not waiting to hear the other person, your primitive brain has taken over. There are times when our primitive brain becomes so powerful that it takes over our more rational brain. At these times we aren't fit to argue well; we risk becoming hurtful and destructive. A fiery argument is not helped by adding our own sparks.

Often a sign this has happened is that you find yourself totally convinced that you are right and feel an almost overwhelming urge to convince the other person of this 'fact'. If this happens you are almost always better off saying, 'I need some time to think about this before I can talk it through well. We are okay, and I need to walk away for a bit and sort it out on my own head first.' Then move away.

The other person will often be furious that you are not continuing the discussion, but it is usually better to walk away so you can get back into the zone and be able to resolve an issue well rather than having a destructive argument.

PROTECT

Pause for a moment and consider that someone you love or like is hurting. Even if it is a complaint that is being directed at you, it is still likely that this person you love or like is in some pain.

As the old saying goes, you can never really understand a person until you have walked in their shoes. Empathy is the ability to put yourself into the shoes of another person, understanding how they see and feel about things. Empathy leads to compassion.

Try it for a moment. Place yourself in your partner's shoes:

- How do they view things?
- What threats might they see?

- What fears might they have?
- What hopes might they have?
- What might they feel reluctant to talk about?

It is useful to consider what might be going on for them. To do this you can use the acronym HALTS:

Hurt – are they feeling hurt, overlooked or disrespected?

Angry – are they feeing angry or frustrated?

Lonely – are they feeling lonely or unloved?

Tired – are they feeling tired, exhausted or overwhelmed?

Stressed – are they feeling anxious?

It may not be wise to ask the other person these questions directly, but considering them yourself will help you to be more compassionate.

HALTS helps you to consider what may be lurking out of sight in the iceberg of the argument.

Let's look again at the diagram showing the key to successful relationships.

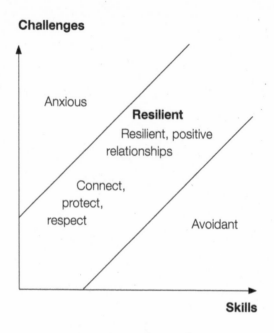

In being responsible for protecting your relationship, your aim is to bring yourself and the person you are in a relationship with back into the resilient zone. In almost all situations your first best option is to listen to the other person. Sometimes that is all you can do. By listening and not rushing to provide a solution, you will often calm someone who is upset. Relationships work best when we soothe one another – not by having answers for other people's problems, but by being there with them and being there for them.

If your partner is agitated you may need to listen calmly and talk quietly about the issue. If they are urging you to provide a response by asking something like, 'Well, what are you going to do about it?' you may have to reply, 'I'm not really sure right now. This is important and I need some time to think it through.'

If your partner is absent and disconnected, see it as a self-protective mechanism on their part. Try not to let their apparent lack of involvement topple you into frustration. It is easy to see disconnected absenteeism as a lack of caring, but it is usually because the person is taking refuge and feels in need of protection.

Once someone has sought the safety of disconnected absenteeism they need to come out and be closer to you in their own time. No amount of rattling the pots in the background or repeated hints or cajoling them into a conversation will work.

If you sit around waiting for them to come closer you will often become frustrated and agitated. And the interesting thing about frustration and agitation is that we usually want to let someone know that we are feeling this way. Despite our best intentions to wait it out and let the person have the space and time they need, we often can't resist expressing our feelings.

You may ask:	The most likely reply is:
Are you okay?	Yes
Is anything the matter?	No
Can I help with anything?	No

Rushing a disengaged, disconnected person back into conversation about a difficult issue is a really bad idea. In fact, it is a sure-fire way of guaranteeing your relationship will be heading into the emergency room with little chance of recovery.

It is also not advisable to rush about trying to fix everything else up for them. While tidying the kitchen, taking out the bin, buying flowers or painting the back room are lovely gestures, you will often be seen as not understanding the real issue. It is best to say something like, 'I know you need some time and space for yourself. I will go and do other things for a while so you can have that time. Please let me know when you would like to talk about this. We will sort this out when you are ready.' Often it is best not to wait for an acknowledgement or provide a farewell kiss – just head off and do something else for a while.

There are some people who close up tighter than a clam with a tube of power glue. They couldn't be prised open with a jackhammer. If you want to remain in a relationship with someone like this, you need to accept who they are.

As mentioned in Step 2, we have four basic choices in all relationships:

1. Stay in the relationship, change what can be changed and live by your values.
2. Stay, accept what can't be changed and live by your values.
3. Stay, give up and do things that make the relationship worse.
4. Leave the relationship and live by your values.

Just you have to accept the way some people are in order to protect your relationships, there are some activities and topics to avoid. Similarly, there are some issues where arguing won't make any difference – the number or quality of ex-boyfriends or ex-girlfriends, and the attributes of your partner's family come to mind as examples.

RESPECT

There is a moment in every ongoing dispute in a personal relationship when we should all pause and think, 'How did I squander all that goodwill in this relationship?'

In relationships you have to know what you want. This means being clear headed about what 'winning' an argument actually means for you. Winning on a sports field and winning in a relationship bear no resemblance to each another. A victory in one setting can be a complete disaster in the other.

When people from two different families come together, the rules and habits of two different tribes of people do not always sync neatly – one says 'tomayto' and the other says 'tomato', as the old song goes. This is not guerrilla warfare in which the winner takes all. If you 'win' too forcefully and completely in a relationship conflict, you lose.

I have sat with many people in my therapy room who thought they had won an argument only to find it cost them half their house, most of their time with their kids and half their life savings.

Whatever is begun in anger ends in shame.

Benjamin Franklin

So arguments are not all-out battles to be won at all costs – they are shared issues that need to be resolved. It is not about dominating and getting your own way, it is about collaborating.

Arguing isn't a great way to convince people. In fact, arguing is useless as a way of changing someone's actions. Reasoning won't carry the day: reassurance and protection will.

Most people make up their minds about intensely emotional issues long before logic has had much chance to kick in. This means that persuasion is almost useless. Instead, help the person to feel comfortable enough to return to the resilient zone so they may be able to consider other points of view.

As reasonable, logical and clear as your issue no doubt is, logic only penetrates when someone feels connected, protected and respected. It is only when we are in the resilient zone that we make good decisions.

The best gift you can give your partner is your ability to be open hearted and respectful. This involves offering our own vulnerability and an intention to protect the dignity of others.

The best gift you can give your partner is your ability to be open hearted and respectful.

Conflict in close relationships is often disheartening. Using CPR is re-heartening. Keep your focus not just on the immediate issue but also on the long-term health of your relationship.

Some people act as if their arguments are like boxing matches where the normal rules don't apply. Gloves are off, knuckles are bared and the winner takes all. This is damaging and dangerous. When you argue in a relationship you are still in a relationship, and what you do in that argument has consequences for your relationship.

Think about how you are at your best. Are you a trustworthy person who can find it in your heart to forgive others, who can be relied on to have integrity, who is generally hopeful about your life and your relationship, and who is compassionate and caring? Even when other people act in shabby or awful ways in arguments, hold true to yourself. Be the good person you are. It is important to convey respect in an argument and essential to be able to respect yourself afterwards.

If you can't hold true to yourself in your partner's company, walk away and regain your composure.

When I talk about this with people in my therapy room they sometimes think I am asking them to give in to anything their partner wants. This isn't the case. It is possible to hold a clear, firm position on an issue without falling into the trap of being destructive or compliant.

You are not the first people in a relationship to have an argument or a difference of opinion. Many people stay in healthy relationships while holding very different opinions about politics, religion and even which sports team to support. Ask yourself: why is disagreement a threat? It is important to hear the fear. We can fear that this issue is so powerful it will end our relationship. Does it really need to?

Ask yourself:

- How do I protect and respect myself?
- How do I protect and respect us?

By calmly taking the time to explore options and consider alternatives without feeling pressured into conceding or defending, we give ourselves a chance to be in the resilient zone and use our creative thinking to devise solutions.

Our best solutions are slow cooked. They take time to infuse and mature. A solution that is hastily decided upon usually backfires just as quickly and often causes flare-ups that worsen the situation.

Together you have solved problems in your relationship. Despite the odds, you have been together and have worked through your differences. It is time to honour the work you have already done and take the time to see whether you can invent a solution that works for this issue and for everyone.

All lives have problems. All relationships have issues. Most of us want better lives and that means taking the time to create better relationships.

Pulse report

There are times when problems overpower our relationships. There are also times when one partner becomes disheartened and disillusioned. This is when conflict can poison even the best of relationships. Learning how to contribute, to be with the other and to resolve issues as they arise means being able to care fully for yourself and your partner. This empowers us all to create, foster and nurture a love-filled life.

Never ever do these in a dispute …

- Never tell the other person they are overreacting; instead, acknowledge the upset and resist the temptation to defend a position.
- Never threaten with ultimatums.
- Avoid making off-the-cuff diagnoses or conducting character assassinations.
- Don't bring in tangential issues or up the stakes.
- Don't tell them not to think about it, or that they are blowing the issue out of proportion.
- Don't think you can joke your way out of it.
- Never try to ignore or argue with someone's perception; instead, try to understand it. If we can try to understand when someone has a different point of view rather than convincing them to change their view, we can resolve the issue.
- Don't add in past issues or hurts. The past is the past and unless you raised it at the time, treat past issues as being passed their expiry date.

ASSESS THE PULSE OF YOUR RELATIONSHIP

Where are you up to? Are there signs of progress? Are there areas you need to work through again? Is your relationship:

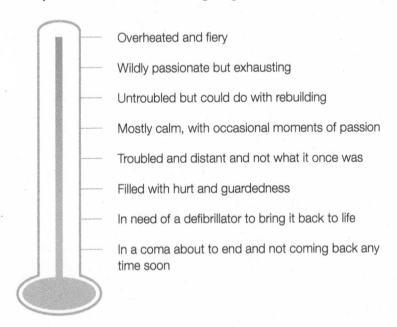

Overheated and fiery

Wildly passionate but exhausting

Untroubled but could do with rebuilding

Mostly calm, with occasional moments of passion

Troubled and distant and not what it once was

Filled with hurt and guardedness

In need of a defibrillator to bring it back to life

In a coma about to end and not coming back any time soon

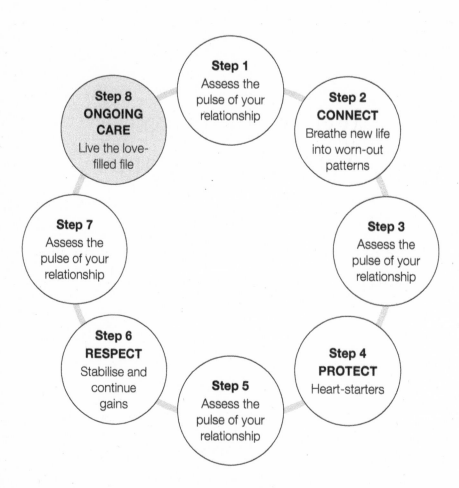

CPR model: Connect, protect and respect

ONGOING CARE
LIVE THE LOVE-FILLED LIFE

Why issues and arguments become 'loopy': Ladder climbers and tapestry weavers

A few years ago I was delivering a keynote speech at a conference for the female heads of multinational companies. The room contained 120 of the most powerful women in the country. Before I even started my presentation, a hand shot up to ask a question: 'Before you begin, Andrew, could you please tell us your view of women and leadership in organisations?'

As I said, these were powerful women. I paused before I answered, as my presentation wasn't specifically on women and leadership. 'Women in leadership,' I started out tentatively, 'are often like tapestry weavers who imbue themselves into the very thread and weave of an organisation, strengthening the tapestry as they go. Too many men climb the ladders of a corporation and sit at the top pounding their chests and feeling important, but the risk is that they may not always have the organisation's trust or support.'

Over the subsequent years I have had the chance to reflect on these words as I've sat with many couples in my therapy room, and the distinction between tapestry weavers and ladder climbers has crystallised in my mind.

'Loopy' arguments and what to do about them

War can erupt in even the most beautiful fields. Even the most wonderful relationships have times of conflict. Some relationships, however, have arguments that spin around and around, like a washing machine cycle on spin dry.

Even the most wonderful relationships
have times of conflict.

The issues keep looping back around and grinding down each person involved. Over time this depletes both people and causes bickering and stress. There is a retreat away from the connect, protect, respect zone into either agitation or absenteeism. As you will recall from the key to successful relationships diagram on p. 68, when we are either highly agitated or absent we can't learn. We can't listen. We can't resolve problems. Misinterpretations occur and mistakes are made.

If you spend a lot of time as a couple in the anxious or avoidant zones you will often feel hurt or insulted before the other person has finished speaking. Interestingly, it's not that the problem is difficult to solve that usually causes this; it's that the people involved can no longer see each other's points of view.

Ladder climbers and tapestry weavers

We can think of some people who are primarily ladder climbers and others who are primarily tapestry weavers. The ladder climbers find it hard to fit more than one person on each rung, so one person needs to be further up, and therefore more powerful, than the other. Tapestry weavers like to put out threads of connection and sit at the centre of their weave. There are advantages and disadvantages to both ways of being.

Ladder climbers can have a strong sense of justice. They often have one main mission or purpose in their lives. Usually they are more focused in their social groups and have a few important relationships. Motivated and determined, they are set up for achievement and action, and don't have a lot of time for emotions or consultation. They often value being respected over being trusted.

Tapestry weavers have almost entirely different priorities. They have multiple missions. They have their own purpose, plus a lot of other people's purposes. Tapestry weavers care for a broad range of people. Tuned into other people's lives, they may hold off accomplishing their own projects in order to make sure people are cared for.

Now, before you start thinking that the ladder climbers are just a bunch of heartless overachievers and the tapestry weavers are lovely, warm and fuzzy, we actually need a bit of balance.

Ladder climbers get things done. Some are quite happy to have other people climb ladders too. They can enjoy the beauty of the tapestry even though they may not understand why it is important.

Being at the centre of the tapestry can be more about enabling others rather than directly accomplishing things yourself. Being so tuned into everyone else can make decisive action difficult and inclusivity can be valued over expertise. When everyone's opinion is important, prioritisation can also be difficult. Who is right when everyone is right?

Tapestry weavers might be able to appreciate the advantages of ladder climbing and may at times be able to feign interest in it, but they aren't particularly interested in climbing ladders. They develop more distributed and complex relationships, and link people together. Some tapestry weavers enter into a secret pact: they will sit at the centre of the weave but expect that everyone else will appreciate the sacrifice they are making by being there.

This trade-off doesn't always work out well. Watching other people shine in your own tapestry can be a bit galling, and not feeling appreciated for your contribution can lead to bitterness and feeling overlooked.

Being at the top of the ladder isolates you from the web; being at the centre of the web means you can only ever be halfway up the ladder. And what feels safe for one can feel dangerous for the other.

It is hard for tapestry weavers and ladder climbers to understand each other. For example, why do you spend so much time up that ladder while I'm here looking after this tapestry? Well, all the time I spend climbing this ladder gives you the freedom to look after the tapestry! Here's a scenario:

Ladder climber: You wouldn't believe what a tough day I've had out there climbing ladders.

Tapestry weaver: I know. I'm exhausted too. It's been tough here in the web. Sally has had a cold, Jimmy has a big school assignment to finish and I haven't had a moment to myself.

Ladder climber: What have I got to do to get some appreciation around here!

Tapestry weaver: I was just trying to tell you what's been going on.

Relationships can work best, and worst, when a ladder climber and a tapestry weaver are involved. At its best, the strengths of both approaches strengthen the relationship. At worst, the combination causes 'loopy' arguments. It is hard for tapestry weavers and ladder climbers to change their ways. They often feel obligated to keep doing what they are doing and don't really want to change it.

With two tapestry weavers, one will often be given the ladder-climbing role, or there can be some jostling over who is really at the centre of the tapestry. Two ladder climbers can be fantastically productive but can vie for who is further up the ladder, who is progressing fastest or who is making the biggest contribution

Tapestry weaving can be invisible to ladder climbers. They may not value all the weaving and connecting going around them, mainly because they don't see it. Attempts to connect may completely pass them by.

Tapestry weavers can have their blind spots, too. They may not value all the work that goes into climbing that ladder and how perilous the prospect of being 'taken down a rung or two' can be. So what is the solution?

Everyone makes a different contribution. We all bring our own gifts to our relationships and we usually do the best we can. Relationships often flourish when we have an ethos of care – when we practise CPR.

Who not to fall in love with

Sex can bring problems and complexities, but as a source of troubles love is in an arena all of its own. Falling in love with the wrong person can waste years of a person's life, rob them of their youth and harden their heart with disappointment.

Love is about as rational as a herd of goats in a fine furniture store. We humans get swept up in the moment. This is why it is so important to think clearly about relationships.

In their fantastic book *Families and How to Survive Them*, Robin Skynner and John Cleese discuss the concept of 'the screen', which is similar to Carl Jung's concept of the 'shadow self' mentioned earlier and is a great way of thinking about these quite complex issues.[13] The world of attraction is beguiling. We all have aspects of ourselves we aren't so fond of; we'd prefer that the world didn't really get acquainted with them. We put these parts behind 'the screen'. Then we go out and meet people, become attracted to them and hook up. But whom we desire is not so random. We often find ourselves drawn to people who appear to have strength in an area in which we feel deficient.

For example, if I am anxious and want to be 'calmer', I'll hide my fears and feel attracted to someone who appears calm and confident. It may take me quite some time to discover that the reason they appear to be confident is that they too have placed their insecurities behind their screen.

This is why people from violent upbringings who resolve never to be violent sometimes find themselves attracted to people who appear calm and peaceful but who have a ferocious temper behind their screen.

Those we decide to spend time with and those we choose to stay away from powerfully determine our happiness. In both romances and friendships there is an essential skill in creating satisfying relationships: the capacity to see the world from someone else's point of view. Two further points that apply equally to friendships and romances:

- in any relationship, we are only entitled to receive what we are prepared to give
- the best guide to someone's future behaviour is their past behaviour.

The idea that you can change someone's ways through your own influence is a very, very long bet.

Personality types to avoid

LEECHES

These vacuums seem to have no life of their own and seem to suck the oxygen out of the air around them. They are emotional vampires.

DRAMA QUEENS AND KINGS

These people create relationships that resemble the latest series of any soap opera. They describe themselves as poetic, passionate, artistic. The rest of the world describes them as pains in the rear end.

If you observe this pattern of high drama over some time, listen to the warning bells.

BULLIES

These people take advantage of vulnerable people – they can be directly belittling and intimidating or neglectfully inconsiderate and hurtful. They could be racists, intellectual snobs or superior social climbers.

Be especially wary of anyone who is prepared to be cruel to animals. This often indicates an inability to consider life from another's point of view.

CLING-ONS AND DROPKICKS

These people don't so much have a friendship group as a mobile welfare agency. They spend much of their time rescuing others, even when they don't particularly need rescuing. By associating with the needy they can feel reassured, safe and wanted.

At first they can appear to be helpful, admirable people and then you begin to wonder if the lives they seem to be saving are really in need of saving.

SPOTLIGHT HUGGERS

These people seem to think they are the centre of the universe. As soon as the focus shifts away from them, they do something – anything – to regain attention. Their attention grabbing behaviours can include elbowing others aside, humour, distraction and even having a mishap or accident.

This demand for attention is often accompanied by self-absorption. They find sharing the floor with people difficult, listening to them a bother and caring for them a waste of their time.

Some of these people are chronically late. Sometimes this is just a wayward lack of organisational skill but when it is a pattern you may also consider the possibility of thoughtless self-absorption.

PEOPLE WITH LOTS OF ENEMIES

Remember, the best predictor of future behaviour is past behaviour. If you meet someone with a bunch of enemies, a series of fraught friendships and a litany of discarded relationships, first assume they have been unfortunate. If you observe that they seem to spend a lot of time discussing the people who have done them wrong, they may be on the road to becoming a hater.

SUBSTANCE ABUSERS AND ADDICTS

People who use illegal substances tend to use other people as well. Not all substance-abusing people are relationship dynamite, but if the drug use continues, start to worry. If you think there might be a problem, there probably is.

This group also includes habitual gamblers, sex addicts and people who squander other people's money for their own pleasure or needs. Failing to take responsibility for your own wellbeing means it is unlikely that you will be able take care of the other people in your life.

Being the person your partner wants to love

Think about yourself when you are at your absolute best in relationships. That's the sort of person you would like to be involved with. If you were asked to draw up a list of attractive personality traits, you might include some of the following:

- kind
- trusting
- forgiving
- acting with integrity
- hopeful and positive
- compassionate and caring.

We all hope our love will be like a tango: hot, sultry and lusty at times, slow and smooth at times and sensuous at others. Instead, what we mostly get is two people stumbling around trying to synchronise their lives.

This is like being with your partner at a fancy ball where you are expected to dance. Neither of you remembers all the dance steps, so you make your best attempt at covering up for the missteps of the other by accommodating them and hoping in turn that they will conceal and forgive your most glaring errors. At best, as the two of you lurch along, you quietly giggle with each another and share the joke of putting on a better show than either of you would alone. After a while you forget about trying to make a good impression and have a great time.

Being the person your partner wants to love is a lot about helping you both stay in the resilient zone. This doesn't mean a placid, humdrum life. It means livening things up and being passionate, and also having the intention of living a great life together.

Clearly life gets busy, so if you don't plan times when you will be happy and enjoy yourselves, work and other demands can dominate. This takes clear, determined intentionality.

Don't play to win, play to be happy. When problems arise (as problems always will), discuss them sooner rather than later. It is always easier to solve small, 'fresh' problems than big, 'stale' ones. Talk with the intention of resolving them rather than 'winning'.

Love is a feeling. Feelings are changeable. Feelings are prone to being buffeted by circumstances. Love is also about the art of enchantment. In addition to being present for your partner, help them to feel special. Find ways of enchanting them.

In a way, each successful relationship requires that we concoct a 'recipe' for love. At regular intervals we need to cook up a new batch because our supplies can dwindle. I rather like the following recipe, created by British journalist Jemima Lewis.[14] She believes each month should include:

- 2 romantic walks
- 2 romantic gifts
- 3 home-cooked romantic meals
- 1 breakfast in bed
- 2 dinner dates

- 7 cosy nights in
- 1 trip to the pub
- 1 trip to the cinema
- 6 proper conversations

Have a think about what your recipe for a romantic month would be. Ask your partner. Share your ideas.

Whatever seems to be your own ideal recipe for a loving month, it will involve times of closeness. Sharing deep conversations and doing things in synchronicity with others builds intimacy and trust. We are built to harmonise with the people around us. From our very first moments of tracking and then imitating our parents' faces we are in sync with other people. It is how we learn to connect with others and how we soothe ourselves.

An interesting 1997 study by American psychologist Professor Arthur Aron and others explored whether intimacy between two strangers could be accelerated by having them ask each other a specific series of personal questions.[15] The 36 questions are broken up into three sets, with each set intended to be more probing than the previous one. You might like to use these questions or topics in conversation with your partner.

SET 1

- Given the choice of anyone in the world, who would you want as a dinner guest?
- Would you like to be famous? In what way?
- Before making a telephone call, do you ever rehearse what you are going to say? Why?
- What would constitute a 'perfect' day for you?
- When did you last sing to yourself? To someone else?
- If you were able to live to the age of 90 and retain either the mind or body of a 30-year-old for the last 60 years of your life, which would you want?
- Do you have a secret hunch about how you will die?

- Name three things you and your partner appear to have in common.
- For what in your life do you feel most grateful?
- If you could change anything about the way you were raised, what would it be?
- Take four minutes and tell your partner your life story in as much detail as possible.
- If you could wake up tomorrow having gained any one quality or ability, what would it be?

SET 2

- If a crystal ball could tell you the truth about yourself, your life, the future or anything else, what would you want to know?
- Is there something that you've dreamed of doing for a long time? Why haven't you done it?
- What is the greatest accomplishment of your life?
- What do you value most in a friendship?
- What is your most treasured memory?
- What is your most terrible memory?
- If you knew that in one year you would die suddenly, would you change anything about the way you are now living? Why?

- What does friendship mean to you?
- What roles do love and affection play in your life?
- Alternate sharing something you consider a positive characteristic of your partner. Share a total of five items.
- How close and warm is your family? Do you feel your childhood was happier than most other people's?
- How do you feel about your relationship with your mother?

SET 3

- Make three true 'we' statements each. For instance, 'We are both in this room feeling ...'
- Complete this sentence: 'I wish I had someone with whom I could share ...'
- If you were going to become a close friend with your partner, please share what would be important for them to know.
- Tell your partner what you like about them; be very honest this time, saying things that you might not say to someone you've just met.
- Share with your partner an embarrassing moment in your life.

- When did you last cry in front of another person? By yourself?
- Tell your partner something that you like about them already.
- What, if anything, is too serious to be joked about?
- If you were to die this evening with no opportunity to communicate with anyone, what would you most regret not having told someone? Why haven't you told them yet?
- Your house, containing everything you own, catches fire. After saving your loved ones and pets, you have time to safely make a final dash to save any one item. What would it be? Why?
- Of all the people in your family, whose death would you find most disturbing? Why?
- Share a personal problem and ask your partner's advice on how they might handle it. Also, ask your partner to reflect back to you how you seem to be feeling about the problem you have chosen.

What questions would you add?

Getting through the rough to get to the smooth

There is an interesting phenomenon that occurs in cooperation between partners after experiencing relationship problems. In their 1965 study, researchers Rapoport and Chammah found that in 300 interactions, slightly less than 50 per cent of people were cooperative the first time the issue occurred.[16] This then dropped to 40 per cent until the 30th interactions and then steadily increased to 75 per cent. In the last 25 interactions the partners made the same choice.

What this indicates is that there is value in calmly talking things through. People may start out fiercely in disagreement and this may intensify as their differences are aired. If we can sit through the heart of the dispute and continue to discuss the problem, we tend to move towards synchronicity and agreement.

Helping your partner become the person you love to be with

This book opened by observing that love puts magic in your eyes. There are processes we can all learn to create that magic. The enchantment of someone else is an art form. It fills the other person with delight and wonder. This is not about being inauthentic or deceitful; it is about creating a new world of possibility with someone.

The fine art of friendship

Of course, friends and romantic partners are not the same, but if we treated our romantic partners like we treat our most treasured friends we would often be in a better place. While the intensity of early love is beautiful, to have a successful long-term relationship we also need to develop friendships with our partners.

To have a rewarding life, cultivate friendships. Classical Greek dramatist Euripides, who perhaps may not have had the happiest home life, wrote in *Alcestis* that, 'One loyal friend is worth ten thousand relatives.'

Wonderful relationships have great passion and great friendship. No relationship shows the power of forgiveness more than friendship. A longstanding friendship involves an implicit agreement: 'I'll overlook and forgive your faults if you'll overlook and forgive mine.'

Connect

Relationships based on great friendships last for life. These are the people you choose to have in your life.

Stay connected – share ideas, jokes, news; don't allow life to let you drift apart. There is work involved in building and maintaining a friendship, and there has to be an investment from both sides in order for it to work.

You don't need to compete with a friend; they are already on your side. Have integrity, stick to your word. Being unreliable will make your friends think twice before asking you for something. When in doubt, say yes to their invitations. Try to be somewhere when you say you will be there. Punctuality is important. Expecting friends to wait for you conveys disrespect.

Ask your friends for help. Doing so and being appreciative will build your friendship because you've shown that person that you need them.

Your romantic partner can be your best friend but probably shouldn't be your only one. And it is unwise to let your romantic partner choose all your friends.

Protect

In a world that seems to treat people as expendable and interchangeable, it is wise to cultivate friendships both with romantic partners and in the world. It is important to have a few people who will stick by you no matter what.

Respect

Look to relationships with others as one of your best sources of happiness. Praise and encourage generously – search for the positive aspects in other people, because if you look for the best, you will often get the best.

As the Roman philosopher Seneca once said in his Moral Letters to Lucilius, 'If you wish to be loved, love. Give more than you get and you will get more than you give.'

PART TWO

RELATIONSHIP ESSENTIALS

CPR FOR WOMEN AND MEN
REVOLUTIONISING THE MESSAGES FROM YOUR PAST

We are living at a time of great possibility. Wherever you see yourself on the gender and sexuality spectrum, you have many more options than your parents ever did. And you have options your grandparents couldn't even conceive of. You can enjoy greater diversity, flexibility and fluidity of identity than any other previous group of humans has experienced.

What is most exciting is that this will revolutionise how we define ourselves and how we relate to one another. As with any great shift in human relationships, though, there is the possibility of confusion as well as opportunity. It is time to be aware of the echoes of the past – but not to be defined by them.

The intention of this section is not to perpetuate gender stereotypes, but to overcome them. Let's discuss some common relationship messages from the past that seem no longer suited to our world. These are like echoes – it can be hard to work out their origins. The messages they send can prevent people from entering into new revolutionary possibilities for their relationships. But through awareness comes freedom of choice.

The lies your ancestors told you about love

In the previous chapters we discussed the traditional distinction of tapestry weaving and ladder climbing, and how these approaches can create different worlds and misunderstandings. Being aware of these patterns is useful. Knowing that you can transcend them is liberating.

One of the great gifts of social media is that we can all be both tapestry weavers, builders of extensive networks, and ladder climbers.

It is often the case that we succeed more sustainably when we *all* succeed. Old ideas of meritocracy and hierarchy, where success is a limited commodity enjoyed by a few, may be giving way to ideas of success through networking.

Ranking, segmenting and specialising human potential may have served an industrial model of human relationships, but no longer applies in a world in which contributions can come in many different forms, from all types of people, with all types of backgrounds.

Now, you may be thinking, 'What has all this got to do with how my relationship works?' Well, let's identify a few messages from your ancestors – echoes from the past, if you like – and see whether they apply to, or even limit, you.

Purposeful planning beats presence

The traditional idea of looking to the future in case of tough times ahead makes sense. However, it can often translate into a 'someday' mindset. This usually goes along the lines of 'Someday when I am [rich enough/fit enough/popular enough/loved enough/successful enough etc.] I will be able to [live in perfect harmony/retire/go on the trip of a lifetime etc.]'. In the long term, this can result in spending our lives chasing the end of a rainbow that we never reach.

Some women who have absorbed this echo of the past waste considerable portions of their lives worrying about relationship issues that never actually happen. Some men who have absorbed this echo of the past waste considerable parts of their lives completing tasks that don't need to be done. Some men and women do both.

Successful relationships are about presence. It is hard to be intimate with someone who isn't there. When you choose presence in the company of others over achievement for yourself, you will lead and inspire your partner powerfully and positively.

Successful relationships are about presence.

Difference equals danger

For much of the past, differences were fearful things. The world was divided between races, sexual orientations, women's issues, men's issues and more. Today, we know enough to recognise that these 'categorised' issues are, in fact, all human issues.

This doesn't mean we should diminish differences between people. Instead, we should avoid categories and stereotypes, and celebrate that each of us is a gift with a unique contribution to make. After all, we now recognise that our brains are as unique as our fingerprints. No one else has your intricate web of neuronal connections.

This makes comparisons pointless. Become as much of *you* as you can – not in a self-absorbed, full-of-yourself kind of way, but so you can bring as much of yourself as possible into the relationships you create, and so you can contribute to them in your own way.

It's about getting it right

In the past, doing things in the 'right' way was highly valued. It still is. I remain fond of the pilots of the planes I fly in, who land in the right way at the right airport, and I like my dentist to fix the right tooth.

But if we apply this idea of doing things right too strictly to human relationships it can create a tyranny of conformity. It can stifle lives in a time when there are many and varied ways of achieving outcomes.

In the past girls especially were often socialised to do the 'right thing'. Competence at tasks by mothers was often seen as a demonstration of love within families. The message that was delivered was, 'If I get it right I will be loved'. A loved daughter was equated with being a successful and productive one. Love then equalled pleasing others and not upsetting anyone.

This can lead to conformity and compliance. For example, in the #MeToo movement we hear stories of women 'freezing' in the face of dreadful abuse and being unable to speak up about behaviour they were unhappy with. We also hear of men who, rather than questioning the belittling comments made about women from work colleagues, prefer to remain silent so they don't upset anyone.

To revolutionise relationships we need people to learn to speak up and out about injustice and abuse. We need people who can speak up to keep themselves and others safe and protected. If ever there is a time to rip up the 'rule book' of relationships rather than sit by silently for fear of upsetting anyone, that time is now.

It's not okay to have emotional baggage

On the dance floor of love, you may have had many victories, but may have also been scarred. You may have hurt others and have been hurt in return. Such wounds of the heart can create restricted and repetitive ways of safeguarding yourself that can imperil relationships. Like it or not, intimacy requires vulnerability, and vulnerability means risking having your heart broken. Some men are socialised to 'play it cool', remaining distant or uninvolved. Some women are socialised to play 'hard to get'.

If you are struggling to create close, intimate relationships, go through the process of reviewing why the relationships you've had have ended. Ask yourself, 'What was my role in that relationship ending?'

Don't say what you want

Many wonderful relationships never get a chance to develop due to reticence and shyness, and because one person is waiting for the other to show interest.

In the past, women were often socialised to be indirect in their communications. Their softer, sometimes more apologetic, style of communication usually worked better than the pointed, focused style of many men. In many cases it is highly effective, but a softer communication style can also have its downsides – messages intended directly can be received as uncertain, or as hints or suggestions.

The classic example is of a woman who is a passenger on a long road trip and as the car approaches a roadside stall, she asks her partner, 'Would you like to go to the toilet?' 'No,' her partner replies, 'I'll drive on for a while.'

The woman spends the next hour busting to use the toilet, fuming silently.

Learn to make direct requests and suggestions. If you like someone, let them know. There is no need to feel ashamed about it. Once you have told them, wait. What they decide to do with that information is up to them.

They should know what I want

One of the great traps, or echoes from the past, is the idea that if someone really loves you they should know what you want and what you think. The crazy idea was that 'true' love conferred onto your partner special telepathic powers. Having a soulmate is great; having a mind reader is just scary.

The world is such a busy place that people often don't tune in to each other well. They don't always pick up feelings of sadness or anxiety. You need to tell them what your attachment needs are. If you need time and space, tell them. If you need hugs and cuddles, tell them.

Arguments solve problems

The old idea that a heated exchange of words and viewpoints is the best way to solve a problem or convince someone about something probably never had much validity. It has even less now.

If you think back to our diagram about the anxious, resilient and avoidant zones on page 68, you'll remember that in the midst of arguments we are often anxious and/or avoidant, meaning we are not listening or thinking constructively.

If you really have to have an argument, do so. But then make it a priority to solve the issue soon after. In a world of distractions, we can act as if our relationship problems are solved when, in fact, we can forget or overlook them. You might find the PICCA method of decision making, described on pages 188–93, helpful in such cases.

A relationship needs both people to carry it

While generally relationships work best when two people share the responsibility for being involved, this is not always the case. There will be times when the gentleness between you hardens and hurts become so deep that little love is present. There will be times when you or your partner will lose your sense of belonging and togetherness. At these times it will be up to you to reach out – gently, tentatively – to connect, protect and respect your partner. In tough times, having just one person healing the relationship is enough.

Respect is earned through success

In the past, respect was often earned through heroic efforts or achievements. Having smart kids, getting a flash car, being in a good job and wearing stylish clothes were markers of someone who had 'made it' and was worthy of respect.

Respect comes not from being able to swim further, jump higher, work harder or earn more money than anyone else. That will gain you accolades and sometimes envy. If you are not careful, it can even give you a heart attack.

Respect is gained by being connected and appreciating other people. When you are in the presence of a respectful person, everyone feels smarter, funnier and more liked. Respect is gained by giving rather than acquiring.

Don't be too loving

In the past a lot of derogatory terms were thrown at people who expressed their love too openly: 'needy', 'dependent', 'neurotic', 'clingy' and 'high maintenance'.

Some people often want to hide the depth of their feelings as if they are embarrassed about their emotions. A person who allows themselves to love openly and grandly frees themselves. Love allows you to sneak past your own ego and loving well frees people from envy. Love enables you to want the best for others.

The more you love, the less you need to control anything. You experience everything deeper and slower and more lovingly.

Love will complete you

In the past, romantic notions were that you would find a partner and they would complete you. Hopefully your partner *will* enrich your life and broaden your experiences, and provide a safe platform for you to explore the world more deeply. Nevertheless, it is best for *you* to take on the responsibility of completing yourself.

People need to have a clear relationship with their purpose and their work. Most of us spend as much time working as they do with their families or friends. The poet David Whyte points out that work is like a marriage in that you put up with a lot, you spend a lot of time together and you are mostly devoted to it.

Respect is more important than love

In the past the world raised many children through a system of shame and blame. Messages like 'You've let us down and you've let yourself down' distorted people's view of respect.

Some men would prefer to be unloved than disrespected, whereas some women endure feelings of inadequacy and disrespect in order to feel loved. In order to feel respected, you need to respect yourself.

When you feel disrespected it is likely that you get angry. This is because you care. But no one respects someone who loses control, who becomes abusive or violent. If you feel unable to manage the times when you feel disrespected, get some independent professional support.

If it helps, think about this like getting your car serviced or your teeth fixed. Very, very few people in the world are their own mechanics and also do self-dentistry. Just as you call in specialists to help with certain areas, seek out assistance for emotional areas if you are struggling to manage them.

Once you are 'in' a relationship you can relax

Changing your status from 'single' to 'in a relationship' should be a signal to you to attend more, not less.

Ask yourself, 'What did I do originally that made me irresistible?' Be interesting and, above all, be *interested* in your partner. Notice and remark upon their intellect, wit and strengths. Express and display your desire for your partner. Help your partner feel special and they won't just hold a candle for you, they'll light up sparklers.

The revolutionary invitation

This book is an invitation to you to create a future form of relationship, one that is not bound or constrained or even defined by the above echoes of the past, but one that connects, protects and respects each person in it.

Connect by making proposals

Consultation is good but sweeping partners off their feet is better. Invite your partner into a world of fun. Rather than offering a humdrum invitation such as, 'Do you want to go out for dinner?' instead say, 'I've found a fantastic restaurant that I think you will love, let's go.'

Surprise gifts have more power than scheduled ones. No matter how sensible and practical a domestic gift appears to be to you, never, ever give a partner a dishwasher, a vacuum cleaner, a spanner set or a washing machine as a present for their birthday.

Protect through touch

In the past, some people didn't touch each other much and in some cultures it is still actively discouraged – so much so that touching comes to signal, 'They want sex'.

We live in a world that bombards people with sexualised messages and, as a result, people can become reserved and wary of touch. People are often fearful of the meaning of touch, but at the same time are 'touch-hungry'.

Be the antidote to this for your partner. Notice how much touch they like and be open to hugging them just to enjoy a hug.

Protect and go beyond yourself

Don't give pinched compliments. Be expansive. Develop a range of friends and interests. Too many people fail to value friendships sufficiently or stop making friends when they leave school.

If overreacting to feelings of disrespect is a risk, having a range of interests and friendships is an antidote.

In love it is always best to be open hearted and full of compliments.

Some people feel that to maintain some independence, they need to hide their passions and emotions. This often creates a sense of withholding, which in turn can lead to partners becoming anxious about disconnection.

The cycle in some relationships of one withholding their emotions and the other withholding their respect can easily be overcome by consciously becoming fully appreciative of your partner.

Respect and add value

The world often seems to demean and devalue people. To differentiate yourself, be someone who values others. Be kind and caring.

THE LOVE-FILLED LIFE
KEEPING UP A CULTURE OF CARE

We are all in the care of each other. The purpose of CPR is to create a culture in which we care for one another so that we can thrive and have wonderful lives.

Each relationship has its own mini-culture. That culture can be life and love enhancing or belittling and demeaning. The culture of love is one of wonder. We see the best in each other. As I said, love puts magic in your eyes.

The challenges of life – the disappointments, the grinding build-up of hurts and misunderstandings – can tear away at the essence of even the best loves. How we manage the challenges of life powerfully determines the culture of our relationships.

Psychologist Bruce Tuckman worked out that groups (and a couple is the smallest group possible, so at times the most intense group of all) have stages, which can repeat and cycle over and over.[17]

How we manage the challenges
of life powerfully determines the
culture of our relationships.

These stages occur in the following order: couples form and get together, then they storm, then they norm and perform, before that stage of life or the issue they have been dealing with ends. This cycle of stages can repeat in similar sequences over many issues. When the demands of life change – for example, new career opportunities, babies, promotions, moving house, falling out with friends, making new friends, pursuing new interests or dropping old ones – this sequence of stages begins again.

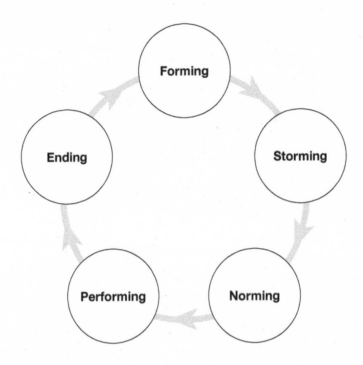

Forming

'Forming' is the first phase described by Tuckman. Forming feels deceptively simple. You have found each other. You are together, a unit, an item and a couple. Love is in the air.

Despite the seeming simplicity of this time, a lot of things are being almost invisibly negotiated as you move from being separate to being together. As the toothbrush moves from one residence to another, subtle rules and guidelines are being laid down:

- Whose friends get priority?
- Which side of the bed do we each sleep on?
- How do we choose where to go out?
- Who cleans up?
- What happens when one person is tired but the other isn't?
- Who controls the remote?

It is a time to set up constructive rather than destructive rules. I remember seeing a couple who had been feeling unsupported by each other for years. They realised that in their earliest days together they had slipped into a pattern of belittling each other in 'joking' ways and that this was tearing them apart. What had felt affectionate and funny in the early stages of love had become damaging in more recent times. By deciding to change their communication pattern they changed their relationship.

As individuals, we all need to realise that some of our ways have passed their use-by date and we need to change. This is the process of maturing.

When a couple forms, two different families' rules, expectations, hopes, dreams and fears are being jumbled together. Mostly things fit well. Then, almost out of the blue, an issue appears and we are storming our way into the next stage.

Storming

There are times for all of us when we yearn for a new conversation and a new way of relating. Even the calmest seas have storms. Just as the relationship moves ahead, it hits a rough stage, which Tuckman calls **storming**. People jostle for control, and the ways these challenges and issues are handled will define the relationship.

Sometimes storms brew gradually. Issues rumble about and discontent builds. At other times a partner unwittingly hits a tender point, causing a flare-up.

Ironically, what often seems to be a couple falling apart is actually a relationship becoming stronger and more authentic, even though it may not feel like it at the time. As each person begins to share their unique contribution, a collision of experiences and preferences occurs. And as these conflicts emerge, we can struggle not only with the conflict but also with how to resolve the conflict.

The risk is that when some couples go into the storming phase they can never figure out how to get out of it. People can revert to strategies they may have used with their siblings. Couples can demonstrate rude and inconsiderate behaviour towards each other and then collect and store their resentments or share them in triangles with others. Friends outside the relationship are invaluable, but don't set them up to be judge and jury about your partner.

Some couples descend into behaviour where love, support and affection are rationed. For example, 'If you make me wait I'll make you wait longer' or 'If you're not going to say "I love you", I won't either.'

You don't need to compete with your own partner. Ask yourself why you would compete with someone who is already on your side. Resist the drift towards mutual competition. This can be a compelling trend if you have had a competitive or combative history with your own siblings.

Storming often occurs in relationships when partners have been too busy or preoccupied to really check in with each another. Storming is a by-product of fragmentation and dehumanisation. One of the ways through this is to think associatively and creatively: think about 'us' rather than 'you and me'. Be aware that this is a time when you can create a better relationship for the future.

In the storming phase, substitute curiosity for judgement. When your partner views things differently from you, try to become curious rather than defensive. Questions take you further than accusations or answers.

This is the time to give-for the relationship. If you become set on 'winning', you lose. It really is that simple. This is the time to argue well and to apply all the CPR principles in this book.

Norming

This is the calm after the storm. There is a ripening of possibility and a crackle of freedom in the air. The relationship becomes cohesive again. New ways of relating are settling. There is now a sense of belonging and camaraderie. There is a shift from 'independence' to interdependence. If the issues have been worked through, the couple can return to the resilient zone and trust one another.

During the norming stage couples make a conscious effort to resolve problems and achieve harmony. There might be more frequent and more meaningful communication and an increased willingness to share ideas. Some couples may begin to develop their own language (nicknames) or inside jokes.

We form patterns in our relationships. Hopefully we create cooperative patterns that hold fast when we hit turbulent times, enhancing joint outcomes and enabling them to be fair for both partners. The expectation is of cooperation and collaboration, not compliance.

Ideally we have norms for caring for one another in, and recovering from, troubled times. Norming is completed when we are clear about our expectations and we've resolved most of the big conflicts – at least for this cycle.

Performing

By this stage the issues have been sorted out in the relationship. Any bickering and jostling for position is over and you are able to have different roles, but also able to change roles when needed. There is flexibility and give-and-take in the relationship.

Trust has been developed partly because in the storming phase no one was demeaned or mistreated. In the performing stage people are aware of their own, and each other's, strengths and vulnerabilities. They are able to see when their partner is anxious or avoidant and help them back into the resilient zone.

Ending

Ending doesn't mean the relationship is over. It means that a phase of life or a major issue has been handled or is completed. Many couples go through different stages: courtship, being a pair, householders, perhaps becoming parents, allowing children more space as they mature, children leaving home and possibly grandparenting. Each stage of life brings a new cycle of forming, storming, norming, performing and ending.

Ending is also about healing. Some issues need to be put into the past so you can create a better future together.

Endings should also connect you with how precious your time together truly is. Sadly, none of us are together forever.

Actively choose the person you are with and keep choosing them. If you can create a relationship in which both of you feel connected, protected and respected, you will love and live well.

THE BREAK-UP RECOVERY GUIDE

Suffering and hurt are feelings none of us wants to have. Heartbreak is something we all hope to avoid and it is also a feeling none of us can avoid. We feel hurt because we love and care. Feeling hurt is a reflection of our ability to love deeply and it is also a sign that we need to recover our sense of who we are.

If we don't transform pain, we transmit it. It echoes and reverberates throughout our lives and our relationships. When we are hurt we are like migratory birds returning in the early spring to find that the nest that we left intact is scattered and broken. Our dreams have been shattered, our hopes have been dashed and our trust has been abused. Slowly we either have to patch up our broken nest or build a new one.

Hurt can help you to move towards
what is right for you.

We think heartbreak only happens when things have gone wrong: an unrequited love, a shattered dream, a hope for the future shredded. Heartbreak is painful but it can also be the start of growth if you let it. Hurt can help you to move towards what is right for you. Give yourself time to gradually unveil what that is.

Recovering from hurt

One way to recover from hurt is to mentally sit beside it as you might beside a close friend in need of comfort. Feel its tenderness and sadness. Perhaps you can relate to its deep sense of disappointment and desolation. Things have not turned out as planned. Love has become a wound.

Just sit with hurt. Let it be there. You can feel deeply, profoundly hurt and sad without being depressed.

Try not to let hurt bubble its way into anger. Anger can temporarily alleviate hurt, but in the end it solves nothing. Anger and blame just lead back to more hurt. Sitting with and gently accepting your own deep sense of hurt will strengthen you. Sitting with hurt eventually takes us towards compassion – for ourselves and for others.

Feelings of hurt poison the best of relationships and can rob us of the best memories of our lives. Hurt can cause a form of temporary blindness. You may know people who, after a relationship ended badly, become blind to the gifts and the good parts of that relationship. Left to fester, hurt can become bitterness, resentment or even self-hatred. It can entrench itself and divide your heart.

Learning from a past relationship is partly about realising what not to do next time, but it is also about not forgetting what went well in that relationship.

Don't try to change or cure your sense of hurt. It is an appropriate feeling after all that has happened. As you sit beside your own hurt, use it to forge your resolve. Use it to gather the energy and the compassion you need to build a better life.

Avoid trying to influence outcomes

No persuasion, no coercion, no consequences, no influence. For the time being let the situation be what the situation is. Let the other person be who the other person is. As painful as you may find someone else's actions, they are their actions.

Act for the good of others

Use your feelings of hurt to act for the good of others. While you have been embroiled in relationship dramas some other important people may have been neglected. If there is someone you know who is lonely, visit them. Connect with good people. If someone needs a compliment, give it. Walk with people. If you want to, let other people know you feel hurt and sad. There is no shame in it. In fact, we all know these feelings at some stage of our lives.

Be true to your word

Be the person you intend to be. Now. Do what you say you will do. Hold yourself to the truth of who you are. Maintain your integrity. In the heat of disputes or the depths of loss your other commitments can fall by the wayside. This is understandable but it also diminishes your reputation. If you have let people down while you dealt with the intensity of the relationship, now might be a good time to make it up to them – even if it is the last thing you feel up to.

Avoid criticism and blame

Give it up. Decide to make no negative comments about anyone. As hard as it seems, move towards forgiveness. Forgiveness, when you are eventually capable of it, will free you. Blame and criticism will embitter and disempower you forever.

Forgiveness, when you are eventually capable of it, will free you.

Soothe your soul

It takes time to resettle yourself after being rattled by hurt. Find ways to calm and nourish yourself. Instead of drinking or eating too much or frantically looking for another relationship, do things that are nurturing for you. Take trips to beautiful places, see good movies, reread treasured books, see good friends, and go for walks. Hurt means you need to take the time to recover.

Be kind

No one likes feeling hurt but it does help us to understand that this is how many people feel much of the time. Hurt makes us feel grounded and humble. It is important not to let this turn into feelings of dejection or hopelessness. Most of the people you meet are going through a fairly tough time, so be kind. Use the hurt you feel to rebuild the quality relationships in your life.

HOW TO FALL BACK IN LOVE

Falling in love is quite easy; it is the staying in love that takes practice. Plan to spend every day falling back in love with your life and with your loved ones. Appreciate them. One of the easiest ways to love someone is feel lucky to know them.

Some people like to make a distinction between 'loving' and 'being in love'. Sometimes this is said dismissively, as in, 'I love them but I'm not in love with them'. Early love is madness, or as Shakespeare labelled it, 'much ado about nothing'.

As love matures there is a ripening, not a lessening. The urgency might have subsided but in its place evolves a deeper, more meaningful connection. Passion and pleasure can intensify.

Love is an emotion. Emotions change over time but you can change your mood and your emotions. In this case, it really is about you. It is time to lift yourself towards love.

Be intrigued. Treat your partner as the mystery they were once. World-famous Colombian author Gabriel García Márquez was once asked about his wife and he replied by saying he had been with her for so long he had not the slightest notion of who she actually was.

Assume that you no longer know who your partner really is and take a week or two to re-learn them. Let your curiosity overrule your judgement.

When Ian Curtis, the lead singer of Joy Division, sang 'Love Will Tear Us Apart' he was right. Life can provide an accumulation of disappointments, hurts and bitterness. Unless we take the steps to connect, protect and respect, it is too easy to drift apart. Then it is time to press the restart button. The rush of life has meant you have probably ignored your relationship and allowed other things to take priority. You need time to rebuild.

What were the things you once did together that gave you such happiness? What was it that made your heart soar?

Sometimes people think if they spend time apart it will help to clarify their desire to be together. Separating to find yourself so you can reunite rarely, if ever, works. Most people need time together rather than time apart.

Consider what would cause you to choose your partner all over again – even knowing what you know now.

HOW TO MAKE A DECISION ABOUT A RELATIONSHIP

We all reach crossroads in our lives where the right direction in which to go forward is not clear. This is true in our lives and it is also true in our relationships.

Most people have never really given much thought to how to make a decision and instead make selections from two options such as, 'Do I stay or do I go?' Your brain wants to keep things as simple as possible. That is why it often narrows things down to one or two choices – this or that, now or later, us or them, here or there, or stay or leave.

While this simple 'one thing or the other' thinking might be okay for most of life, when relationships are difficult or troubled you need to be able to take the time to make clear, rich decisions that are ideally in everyone's interests.

PICCA – a decision-making guide

To know which way to go, you need to make a decision, and to help you remember how to do this you can use PICCA. PICCA stands for a five-step way of making decisions:

1. Problem
2. I wants
3. Choices
4. Compare
5. Act

Problem

The first thing to do is define the problem or decision you need to make. Generally the need for a decision arises when there is a problem. Ask yourself, 'What's the issue?'

At first glance, stating what the problem is may seem very straightforward, but it is also important to get it right. Try out a few different ways of expressing the problem. One way to clarify the problem is to ask yourself five 'why' questions.

For example:

1. I'm worried I don't feel loved in my relationship. Why?
2. We don't seem to make time for one another anymore. Why?
3. We've been working hard, trying to save for a deposit. Why?
4. I feel we need the security of knowing where we can raise children. Why?
5. I think doing anything else would disappoint my parents. Why?

The answer to the final 'why' may be 'Because my parents think I married the wrong person.' As you can see, in this example the problem to be solved shifts, as it often does, from one thing to another. Problems are shifty, sneaky things. What sometimes seems to be the problem camouflages the real problem. Once you have started to identify the problem, move to the next stage.

I wants

These are also known as objectives, but really they are just the things that you want.

Choices

Describe as many alternative ways of getting what you want as you can. Take some time with this. It is often best to come back to the list of choices, three times, adding to it if you can, before moving to the next stage, Comparing. (Interestingly, people find that they develop more ideas standing up than sitting down.)

Often choices we haven't even considered appear if we give ourselves some time to dwell and ponder on the decision. This is why the best decisions take some time. Develop three main choices or directions.

Compare

Go through your list of choices and note which one you'd really love, which one you think has the best chance and which one is a long shot. If you don't have a long-shot option you might want to go back and spend more time developing your choices. A list of choices that looks too practical and realistic can indicate that you have played it too safe.

When making difficult decisions,
there is usually a trade-off.

When making difficult decisions, there is usually a trade-off. This process is usually not a straightforward matter. For this reason it is worth drawing up a comparison table, as described below (see page 193).

Act

The last thing to do is to select an option and act upon it. The means specifying the actions that you will do and developing a timeline for completion.

Let's take a look at the all-too-common problem of work–life balance as experienced by our couple Alex and Robin. Alex wants to revitalise her relationship but fears that she may be rejected. Her partner, Robin, is hardworking and feels they should be working hard and living a frugal life so they can get ahead. The problem is that Alex feels lonely, isolated from her friends and abandoned when Robin spends long hours at the office.

PROBLEM

Should Alex work harder and save faster, take some time to build friendships or reconnect with Robin in a different way?

I WANTS

Alex makes a list of her 'I wants':

- I want to meet new friends.
- I want to have fun.
- I want to feel loved.
- I want to save up and buy a good house.
- I want Robin and I to enjoy each other more.

CHOICES

- Alex could just work hard and put up with feeling sad for a while. Hopefully it won't last forever.
- Alex could plan some new social activities and also try to entice Robin to spend more time with her.
- Alex could run off to Jamaica, join a reggae band and send postcards to Robin in the hope that he will come to find her.

COMPARE

Alex still isn't clear on the decision so she decides to give each activity a ranking based on a five-star system – from five stars for best to one star for worst.

To compare the choices Alex draws up a table:

Wants/activities	Work hard	Find new friends and entice Robin to join in	Run off to Jamaica
New friends	★ ★ ★	★ ★ ★ ★ ★	★ ★ ★ ★
Fun	★ ★	★ ★ ★ ★ ★	★ ★ ★ ★
Feel loved	★ ★ ★ ★ ★	★ ★ ★ ★	★
Save up and get a good home	★ ★ ★ ★ ★	★ ★ ★	★
Robin and I to enjoy each other more.	★	★ ★ ★ ★ ★	★
Total	16 stars	22 stars	11 stars

Alex decides that the attractions of playing in a Jamaican reggae band, while enticing, may place too great a strain on her relationship and ambitions. Given their level of exhaustion, working much harder is not really an option. To make new friends, Alex considers a work-based book club or gym program and even inviting a few colleagues to lunch once a week.

PICCA may not suit the intricacy of every decision that life throws up, but it will give you an opportunity to make more mindful decisions.

HOW NOT TO GET DIVORCED

Times are tough. Your relationship is in the emergency room and the last rites are being read. The person you fell in love with has the capacity and the inside knowledge to destroy you. It is time for drastic interventions.

Divorce has few victors. Children suffer. Everyone, almost invariably, loses. There may be exceptions to this (see the chapter on sinister, demeaning, mercenary or violent relationships) but if you can consider avoiding divorce in your life, do it.

This chapter is about the moment when your partner is on the brink of being out the door or is at the point of turning you out, and it's not what you want.

This is where we reverse the order of CPR. Before you connect again we need to build respect, then protect and then re-connect.

First, if you do not want your relationship to end it is likely you are grieving, hurt and sad. Your partner may want to rush things along to a quick separation. For this reason slow the process down, if you can. Read over the section on hurt and heartbreak (pages 177–82) again.

People who want to end a relationship abruptly are almost always out of the resilient zone. They are either feeling agitated and usually ascribing the reason they feel this way to you. Usually they are in 'flight' mode. Alternatively, they are absent and attributing the reason for feeling deadened to you.

As hard as it is to think about their perspective at this time, it is important. Realise that there is often just as much pain in the person wanting to leave. This can be hard to believe, especially if there has been infidelity, and they will often put on the appearance that they are determined to be rid of you. In the dark recesses of their mind, however, a shred of doubt will always linger.

We are going to use that shred of doubt to increase your chances of not getting divorced.

Respect

The first thing to know is that the person you hope beyond hope will care for you and love you is not able to do that for you at the moment. Even if they don't show it, they are going through their own turmoil and pain. Most likely they are concealing this and instead directing their anger and blame towards you. You may well think, 'Well let them, it's their fault after all – they're the person who wants to leave!'

If you really don't want to separate and divorce, you need to think clearly and be strategic. This means you may need a lot of support from friends and family as you process your feelings.

First, avoid begging, pleading or cajoling. Make sure that the people you vent to or confide in do not make emotional submissions on your behalf.

There is a part of you that is probably hurting like hell. There is probably another part that is furious. The fragile part of you that is in pain wants to cling on. However, if you chase your partner they will feel suffocated or hunted and shift to the agitated zone. They will begin to feel trapped and that everything has to happen quickly. Needing to cope with this will switch them into the avoidant zone. It is time to stop giving your partner a reason to leave you.

This is going to be very hard, but don't be put off by the challenge. It may be the best thing you ever do.

Stop discussing the relationship for a time

Trying to reason with or persuade a partner who wants to end a relationship rarely works. It is never just a matter of convincing the other person. You may be distressed and upset. They are also likely to be confused, reactive and defensive. This situation involves a powerful cocktail of emotions.

Stop pursuing them

Immediately stop anything that your partner might view as trying to keep them involved. This means stopping:

- frequent phone calls, texts, or emails
- loving messages of any kind
- begging, pleading
- describing all the good times in your relationship
- following your partner around
- encouraging talk about the future
- asking for reassurances
- buying them gifts or flowers

- planning holidays or trips away together
- trying to schedule dates together
- the surveillance program – no spying on them, checking their phone or computers or their arrangements.

Stop saying 'I love you.' Completely stop. Every time you say 'I love you', you might be reminding your partner that they may not love you.

Get a life

As shattered as you likely are, get a life. While this is a really big ask, you do need to act as if you are moving forward in your life. Otherwise, you might as well seek legal advice and draw up the documents.

I expect you are asking yourself, 'How can I do this when I feel like crap? I can hardly function, it's a miracle getting out of bed each day, and things are horrible at home.'

Start to treat yourself better. Start doing things that are out of character compared with the way you have been acting lately. Move gently beyond helplessness into action and power.

Be delightful to be with

Allow your mood to be more upbeat in your partner's presence. Appear pleased with yourself and your own life. This is not a 'fake it till you make it' policy, just a 'fake it' one.

During phone calls give the impression that you've handled things; even sound upbeat about life. Don't sit around waiting for your partner to call: get out and do things. Start a new hobby such as rock climbing or ice skating or join a book club or a walking group.

Your partner is most likely getting lots of advice from friends and family. Not all of that advice will be supportive of you. You can't control this. Ignore it as much as possible.

Be unpredictable. Let some of their calls go through to voicemail. During these times, unpredictability and comparative scarceness are your best allies. Being too available and too familiar will be your enemy.

This strategy is not just about playing 'hard to get'. It is the reverse, in fact – it is about being 'easy to be with'. Accept invitations offered by your partner warmly and graciously.

If you attend something with your partner, try not to use that time as an opportunity to discuss your relationship.

Avoid tears and dramatics; enjoy the moments you have with them.

If they are used to you being chatty and sharing your thoughts about your relationship, ask nothing and say little. Simply wish them a good time.

You need to make your partner think that you are going to move on with your life, with or without them.

Protect

Be warm and friendly. Appearing to be getting on with life increases the chances of your partner becoming more interested in you. This strategy won't work for creating a positive relationship but it may save it long enough for you to go back to the start of this book and try some of the methods again.

Taking care of yourself is one of the best things you can do for yourself and your relationship. Teach your partner how to treat you.

Go back to old interests and see past friends. Separating people are not in the resilient zone. Their immune systems may be compromised, so they may be more vulnerable to illnesses and heart attacks.

Do not change your relationship status on social media.

Show respect

There is a Zen teaching story that asks people to hold on tight with an open palm. Sometimes the most powerful way of staying in a relationship with someone is by giving them permission and freedom to leave. By being calm, moving on with your life and being caring of yourself and your partner, you will give your troubled relationship as much chance as it has of revival.

Love is a gift that we give ourselves as much as we give it to other people. The old version of the relationship didn't stand the test of time. If there is to be resurrection of your relationship, it will need to be new, improved and better.

Sit down with a pen and paper and write down all the issues your partner has been telling you about. Take a good, hard look at the list. This gives you the opportunity to create a new relationship.

If, for example, your partner has told you, 'You don't show me enough love', think about how you can be more demonstrably loving. If your partner has described you as moody and difficult, think about ways to begin a more positive life. Let resentments and retributions go. If your partner turns towards you wanting intimacy, have the courage to turn towards them in return.

It is natural for you to want to talk about the relationship. Hold off. Reconnection is tentative. At this time you don't yet have the connectedness or the goodwill needed to strengthen your relationship.

Look your best

Upgrade your appearance. Get a new haircut and a new outfit or two. Start an exercise program. It may not be wise, however, to reconnect with past loves at this time.

Choose happiness over winning

There will be issues of dispute that you can discuss with your partner. Essentially in all our lives we have a choice – do we want to be happy or do we want to win? These are often mutually exclusive and this is never truer than when a relationship is heading for divorce.

If getting divorced will truly make you happier, then do it. If you want to be happy, forget about winning and go for what you want.

Get rid of the mental scorecard

In these times couples often count things: who did the dishes most recently, or how many times I cleaned up last week. Focus instead on the big picture: regaining the relationship you want.

Go to bed angry if you need to

The concept of raising and resolving issues before you go to sleep is ill suited to these times. Hold your tongue, keep your own counsel and resolve to make your own resolutions.

Focus on finances together

Financial pressures can challenge the strongest of relationships. Perhaps debt has got out of control, unemployment is an issue or gambling has been a problem. Try to face these issues together with the help of professionals. Accountants and financial planning services may be a good place to begin.

You have to climb out of a rut to get out of it

You may feel that some or all of the above advice is suggesting you do unreasonable things in order to save your relationship. It will take all of your personal strength to turn the situation around. There are no guarantees of success. It may seem a small consolation but if you end up parting it is important that you did all you could to preserve what once was.

INTO A LIFE OF KINDNESS AND CARING

How well we love dictates to a large extent how well we live.

It determines our joys, our supports, the ways we calm ourselves and each other, our health and to some degree our longevity. As I mentioned earlier, we can only be as healthy as our relationships.

Despite this, the world seems to find many ways of separating us from one another. The pace of life, the depersonalisation of 'social' media and increasing individualistic aspirations all provide more opportunities for us to avoid and disconnect from each other. And when our relationships suffer, we all suffer.

It takes thoughtful determination to create a path that is contrary to the pressures of life. To connect to, protect and respect ourselves and our partners requires purposeful presence.

Life is precious, and it is for living. A well-lived life reverberates with deep, heartfelt intimacy. The sweet touch of a partner's embrace; the rambling conversations with friends, where closeness is more important than content; the light-heartedness of shared laughter. These are some of the treasures of life.

They can be buried or overlooked by the rush of time, by everyday demands and the drive for individual achievement. They can be bought cheaply – imitations that for a moment fulfil some desire, but do not provide nourishment. They can also be lost in the sorrows, losses and setbacks of life, which are part of the journey we all travel through. The shadows of these times can burden us, but there is no need to make them permanent travel companions. Instead, they can help us to value the moments of light, and value the people we share those moments with.

DEALING WITH DANGEROUS RELATIONSHIPS

This section contains advice that may be helpful if you are in a relationship that is dangerous for your physical and/ or psychological wellbeing. I never advocate staying in a sinister, demeaning, mercenary or violent relationship. You are more valuable, more lovable and more wonderful than that, and you deserve much better. You also have the right to determine your own future.

Having said that, it is also important to state that quite a few people decide to stay in sinister, demeaning, mercenary or violent relationships for their own reasons. Relationships are complex. You can love someone but hate what they do.

Other people may treat you badly and then alternate that with treating you really well. These complexities make the decision about staying or leaving difficult.

The person who is best placed to make the decision about staying or leaving is you. Regardless of what friends or family might advise you to do, if the decision you make is not the right one for you, it is unlikely to be a decision you can stick to.

This section is written to support you in making the decision you want to make but also with a view to keeping you safe.

What are the warning signs?

- You feel like you are walking on eggshells most of the time.
- You often feel fearful.
- You do not feel safe in your relationship.
- You feel like you are being taken advantage of financially, emotionally, sexually or physically.
- You feel your partner checks on where you are, not out of caring for you but for jealousy or control reasons.
- You feel neglected and have been feeling lonely in your relationship for a long time.

- You feel isolated by your partner and find it even more difficult to reach out to or talk to other people.
- You worry that if your partner finds out some things about you that they will become uncontrollably angry.
- You have been pushed or hit.
- Your partner has threatened that if you leave them they will kill themselves or someone else.
- You fear that if you don't go along with your partner's wishes, your children, valuable possessions or pets may be hurt or damaged.
- Considerable and unaccountable amounts of money are being withdrawn from joint savings accounts with no explanation.
- Your partner demeans, belittles or insults you.
- Your partner's emotions exhaust you and you don't feel you have any way of influencing them.
- Friends or family have expressed concerns to you about your relationship.
- The relationship is more a duty than a pleasure.
- You stay in the relationship mainly because you fear the consequences if you leave.
- Your partner treats you badly but is sweet and apologises afterwards.

If any of these apply to you, it is likely that you are in an abusive or destructive relationship. This might seem obvious but there are many people who leave relationships and only afterwards realise that they were being abused. It is also important to realise that emotional and psychological abuse can be just as damaging as physical abuse.

Weighing up the decision to leave or stay is the first step in taking care of yourself. Whatever your decision is, it is important to acknowledge deeply that you matter, you can make a decision about this and, as hard and as complicated as it may feel, the decision you make should be respected by others.

If you are at this point, your relationship has not been the one you have chosen. It is not what you wanted. It is not what you hoped it would be. Feeling sad and disappointed and even scared is understandable.

Blaming yourself is never useful. It is time to take better care of yourself. Some questions you might find useful to consider as you're thinking about caring more completely for yourself are:

- Do I want to change my partner? Why?
- Is it my job to change my partner?

- Am I their saviour?
- Have I stopped trusting myself?
- Have I stopped caring for myself?
- Am I trying to change who I am to please my partner?
- Do I want to do this?
- Do I look forward to coming home?
- Do I feel safe in my relationship?
- Do I feel unworthy of someone better?
- Is it worth staying in a relationship because I feel scared of what might happen if I leave?
- Is now the right time to leave?

It is worth taking time to consider these questions deeply.

Relationship choices

As mentioned earlier, with all relationships we have four basic choices.

1. Stay in the relationship, change what can be changed and live by your values.
2. Stay, accept what can't be changed and live by your values.

3. Stay, give up and do things that make the relationship worse.

4. Leave the relationship and live by your values.

Being clear about these choices is harder in sinister or abusive relationships, but even more important.

1. Stay in the relationship, change what can be changed and live by your values

There are many reasons why people decide to stay in abusive relationships. While we can all have our opinions about whether someone should leave or stay, essentially it is a decision everyone needs to make for themselves. Some of the reasons why people I have worked with decide to stay include:

- I feel frightened.
- The children are not the right age.
- It will break my parents' hearts.
- We are in business together.
- My partner can be nasty but it's not that bad.
- I lack the financial resources to leave.
- I fear being lonely.

- They will kill themselves if I leave.
- They will kill me or my children if I leave.
- I have nowhere to go.
- I feel powerless.

Let's accept that you have decided to stay in the relationship. You don't need people tut-tutting and telling you to make a different decision – you need support. Even when one parent is highly dysfunctional, children can be resilient and can function well if they have one parent who loves them and who they can rely on.

One of the dangers of being in a sinister or abusive relationship is being isolated from friends or family. Gradually and safely, the first step is to reconnect with people outside the relationship. You may need to be cautious so as not to give rise to undue jealousy.

Sometimes people in abusive relationships feel so belittled they imagine no one would want to be their friend. This is not true. Reconnecting with people is an important first step to renewing your life.

Earlier in this book I outlined the five main values that underpin positive relationships. Let's revisit them here in relation to sinister relationships.

TRUST

Rebuild trust in some friends or family. If you are away from previous friends, see whether there is a club or activity in your community that you could become part of.

Rebuild trust in yourself. Sinister or abusive relationships shake our sense of self-esteem and self-belief. You cannot rely on your partner to take care of you. You need to look after yourself. You have probably been damaged emotionally or physically by the relationship. This is not something you want for yourself. Take the time to heal and regather yourself. Find time to grieve for the lost hopes in your relationship.

FORGIVENESS

Deciding to stay in a relationship and trying to alter it singlehandedly is a massive effort. It means taking on sole responsibility for everyone in the relationship staying in the resilient zone for as much time as possible.

You won't be able to do this if you are simultaneously giving yourself a hard time. You need to stop blaming and shaming yourself, and give for yourself so you can ultimately decide what is the best action to take.

INTEGRITY

There is no integrity in sinister and abusive relationships. Integrity is about doing what you say you will do and being who you say you are. To give your relationship any chance of revival or survival, you will need to act with impeccable integrity. This may sound unfair, especially if your partner is acting erratically and without any integrity at all.

While you may act privately to ensure the safety of yourself or your children, in your interactions with your partner hold to your own values.

HOPE

Hopes are demolished in sinister or abusive relationships. There is little point staying in and accepting a relationship if it is a barren desert that offers no nourishment or hope. At the very least, start to build hope into your own life. Even if in the beginning it only means small things to look forward to, plan to increase the amount of good things in your life.

COMPASSION

People who have been in abusive relationships often find it difficult to practise self-compassion. Even small acts of self-compassion count, such as getting a haircut, dressing well, calling a good friend or going for a walk.

While you may not feel good about yourself at the moment, in your life people have liked you and loved you. Perhaps trust those people's feelings towards you more than you do your own.

2. Stay and accept what can't be changed and live by your values

In the previous option, you were trying to improve the relationship. This option is more an acceptance of the problems in the relationship, a decision not to try to improve things while also remaining true to yourself.

Your relationship is what it is. It is not what you had hoped for or wanted. Accepting the relationship as it is can lessen your feeling of urgency to improve it.

Deciding to stay in a relationship and accepting that not much can change is heroic. We need to make sure, however, that your heroism doesn't turn into self-sacrifice.

This might involve gently shifting the epicentre of your life. Ideally we place our most intimate relationship at the centre of our lives. Acceptance means no longer doing that and instead focusing on developing other aspects of your life – such as children, family, friends, pets, relatives or work. As much as you can, construct a life for yourself that is fulfilling.

3. Stay, give up and do things that make the relationship worse

This is where you become self-sabotaging. Generally, despite your best intentions, you snipe back, yell back and fight back, often with dire consequences. There is often risk of winning a battle but intensifying the war.

Abusive relationships are not rational. You can't reason your way through them. The common cycle of the abusive person being full of rage then often full of remorse and regret is not usually something you can alter through discussion or reasoning. It is even less likely to be altered through arguing. There may be times when you stand your ground, but be very careful not to endanger yourself.

You either need to leave the relationship absolutely or leave it emotionally enough to not engage in disputes that are dangerous for you. Behind the anger, grief, loss, sadness and disappointment remains a tiny glimmer of hope. Remember, the best predictor of someone's future behaviour is how they have behaved in the past. In this instance, that fragment of hope can be extremely dangerous for you.

Work with a professional who is trained in understanding relationships so that you can emotionally extract yourself to the point where your sinister or abusive partner is not dragging you down to their level.

4. Leave the relationship and live by your values

The final decision to leave the relationship could be sudden, but in reality it is more often a gradual process. Ideally, the first time someone hits or hurts you, you would leave. Life, however, is not ideal and it is not simple.

If you are feeling under threat call emergency services. You should call the police following any violent attack.

Make a safety plan. People who are abusive are often also unpredictable and you never know when you're going to have to get away from them. Creating a safety plan in advance will help you to think more swiftly and clearly during moments of danger. However, do not let a lack of preparation prevent you from leaving if you are in danger.

Set up the emergency or panic function on your phone and set up an emergency alert to be sent to a friend.

Each phone is different, so research the specific functions for your phone within the settings. Enable and personalise your emergency settings so that your location and an audio clipping will alert selected family or friends. When the alert has been received, your family or friends can contact the police on your behalf.

Don't be afraid to contact the police if you are concerned for the safety of yourself and your children.

HAVE A PLANNED EXCUSE

Ensure you have a reason or excuse to leave the house, particularly if you have children and decide to have them leave with you.

KNOW WHERE TO GO AND WHAT TO DO

You may have a relative or friend who can offer you a place to stay for a short period of time. It is worth researching organisations that can assist with temporary accommodation in a safe place.

GATHER IMPORTANT DOCUMENTATION

This includes birth certificates, marriage certificates, copies of accounts and financials. DivorceAnswered.com.au provides a free Separation Checklist for items that you should take or make a copy of. Don't forget to back up documents and emails. Consider giving a copy of, or access to, these files to a person you trust.

STORE HEIRLOOMS AND MEMENTOS

Make sure special or sentimental items of value are located safely outside the house.

HAVE A LEAVING BOX READY

This is handy if you are in a rush, as your key belongings will be with you. The leaving box should include money, keys, keepsakes, certificates, licences, passports, medication, clothes and digital copies of documentation on a USB stick.

This box could be kept at a friend or relative's house. Alternatively, if you do have to leave suddenly and the leaving box is in your home, the police can escort you and supervise while you take your belongings.

SET SOME MONEY ASIDE

If possible, save money into a separate account, as it will make your financial situation easier. Organise pre-payment of expected outgoing expenses. Apply for a credit card and bank account in your own name.

TELL A TRUSTED FRIEND WHAT IS GOING ON

Tell a trusted friend about your concerns and plans. Most importantly, remain in regular contact and ask them to contact police if you fail to make regular contact. It is also useful to have a 'help' word with your friend that notifies them to step in.

Try to be specific with what you would like them to do for you, such as let you stay with them, keep your 'leaving bag', or call the police for you if you give them a 'code word'.

Contact support or government organisations. There are many organisations set up to assist victims of domestic violence.

FIND A SECURE MEANS OF SEEKING HELP

Phone records and call logs can be checked. Computers' browser histories can be traced. To protect yourself, you can try erasing your call log or internet cookies and history. Some browsers also allow you to set them to 'private' mode. If you are still worried that your partner is monitoring your communication with others, you might want to find another computer or phone to use.

Most public libraries offer computers with internet access – this could be a good place to start. You may also want to get a prepaid phone, which could come in handy while looking for help and later when you actually leave.

You could also use a friend's or neighbour's computer or phone. If you need to, make an excuse such as your own computer or phone being broken.

If you are a victim of abuse, find a refuge in your area. They will assist you with resources and guidance.

GATHER EVIDENCE OF ABUSE

Take pictures of injuries, destroyed objects or a room that was trashed during a violent episode; keep bloodied clothing or towels; and collect any documentation about hospital visits due to abuse. Whenever you are injured in an episode of violence, you should seek medical treatment in the emergency room and keep the records.

HIDE AN EXTRA CAR AND HOUSE KEY

If your access to a vehicle is restricted, have an extra key made for your car. If there is already an extra key, hide it in a place you can easily access on your way out. Keep your car ready to leave: park facing out so that you can drive away quickly. Top up your petrol so that you always have a nearly full tank.

KNOW WHERE YOU ARE GOING WHEN YOU LEAVE

If you are going to stay with a friend or relative, choose someone who would not be immediately obvious to your partner.

MAKE A PLAN FOR PETS

You may be able to leave pets with a neighbour or friend, or even take them to a shelter for safekeeping.

LEAVE DURING A SAFE WINDOW OF TIME

Plan and prepare to leave at a time when your abusive partner will be out of the house for a few hours. Give yourself plenty of time to gather your leaving bag and get to a safe place before your partner even realises you are gone.

You do not have to leave a note or an explanation for why you are leaving. Just leave. If you fear that you are in imminent danger, you can have the police pick you up and assist you to leave your home.

DON'T TAKE YOUR PHONE WITH YOU

Store important numbers and contacts in another place. Your phone could be set for tracking without your knowledge. As mentioned above, consider buying a prepaid phone and have it packed in your leaving bag.

CREATE A FALSE TRAIL AFTER YOU LEAVE

If you think that your abusive partner will try to follow you or track you down, think about creating a false trail after you have left. Use your own phone (the one you will leave behind) to place calls to a hotel at least several hours away from your true destination. Use a shared credit card or bank account to prepay for the hotel room you won't use, and have an email confirmation sent to a shared or monitored email account.

You can also book a rental car in the same place or leave a message for a real estate agent and ask them to call you back at your home phone number. Do this just before leaving.

HAVE AN UNLISTED NUMBER AND CONFIDENTIAL ADDRESS

When you have moved to a new home, get an unlisted home phone number. For mail, get a PO box or ask the post office about your state's confidential address program. These steps will make it more difficult to track down your specific location.

If you have children, be sure to talk to them about keeping their home address confidential and not sharing it with your abuser or with strangers. Let their school know about the situation and any access orders that are in place.

CHANGE ALL YOUR PASSWORDS

Any account you have online could be a window into personal information. To be safe, change all your passwords for any account – bank and financial accounts, social media accounts, email accounts and phones.

FILE ASSAULT CHARGES

If you have recently been assaulted or have records of abuse, file assault charges. You might be able to file for assault without physical evidence (particularly if you can provide witnesses to your abuse), but it will be much easier if you collected physical evidence of assault before you left.

GET A NEW COMPUTER

Spyware could be on your old computer, allowing your partner to know everything you do on the computer and read all of your emails. If you can afford to, buy a new computer, or have your existing computer checked by an IT security specialist.

PROTECT YOURSELF AT WORK

Alert your supervisor and the security staff about the history of your relationship and that you have recently left. Remove your number from the office directory, and even change office locations. Ask security staff to walk you to your car.

MAKE SAFETY PLANS WITH YOUR CHILDREN

Teach children what to do if the abusive partner breaks into the house or attempts to kidnap them. You don't want to scare your children, but help them to be prepared. Notify the school or daycare about the danger.

DON'T ISOLATE YOURSELF

Don't park your car in large parking garages or jog at night or in secluded areas. Park as close to your destination as possible.

DOCUMENT EVERYTHING

Keep records of all texts, emails, stalking and harassment. Keep a video or written journal and hide it. Once you are safe and ready, read over the section on recovering from hurt and heartbreak (pages 177–82). Then go through the process of thinking about how your next relationship could be different. By learning how to create relationships that connect to protect and respect people, you will be able to be in a relationship that you deserve.

TAKE THE TIME TO HEAL

After a torrid and abusive relationship, you will need time to reset your equilibrium. You need time to heal. While it can be tempting to seek solace and healing through a better relationship, realise you are wounded in ways that you may not yet know.

One common form of wounding comes from the degree of intensity of abusive relationships. Your relationship has probably bounced from anxious to avoidant and back again with high levels of drama and emotion. There has been very little even-keel or time spent in the resilient zone.

The risk is that you can equate high drama with caring, and calmness with not caring or indifference. As a result you may be at risk of being too ready to form partnerships with people who seem to be exciting and too ready to be bored with people who are calm.

Take the time to recalibrate your own relationship thermometer. Work with a skilled counsellor so that your next relationship is a more positive one. When you are ready, return to the start of this book and plan to create your next relationship – one in which each person connects to, protects and respects the other.

NOTES

1   Research across 200 000 young people and 600
     communities identified the CPR method of promoting
     wellbeing in their relationships. See Fuller, 2017.

2   See Jung, 1957.

3   The Johari Window was created by Joseph Luft and
     Harry Ingham in 1955 ('Johari' is a combination of first
     names).

4   See Rogers, 1995.

5   John Bowlby was a British psychologist who developed
     attachment theory with Mary Ainsworth: see Bowlby and
     Ainsworth, 1951.

6   This is known as active responding: see Gable et al., 2004.

7   See Fredrickson, 2014; Porges, 2017.

8   Stephen Porges' polyvagal theory. See Porges, 2017.

9   Robert Sapolsky, Professor of Neurology and Neurological
     Sciences at Stanford University. See Sapolsky, 2017.

10   These five values were outlined in collaboration with
     my colleagues John Hendry and Neil Hawkes in a series

of unpublished papers on The Relationship Quotient available from www.andrewfuller.com.au.

11 The thinking on the values underpinning relationships stems directly from the work I have been privileged to do with my friends and colleagues John Hendry and Neil Hawkes. I am indebted to and acknowledge and thank them for their wonderful contribution to the five values discussed in this chapter.

12 Sapolsky, 2017.

13 Skynner and Cleese, 2009.

14 Jemima Lewis, *The Sunday Telegraph*, 5 October 2008.

15 Aron et al., 1997.

16 Rapoport and Chammah, 1965.

17 Tuckman, 1965.

BIBLIOGRAPHY

Anderson, J. (1999) *A Year by the Sea: Thoughts of an Unfinished Woman*, Doubleday, New York.

Anderson, J. (2006) *A Weekend to Change Your Life: Find Your Authentic Self After a Lifetime of Being All Things to All People*, Broadway Books, New York.

Appleton, W.S. (1981) *Fathers and Daughters: A Father's Powerful Influence on a Woman's Life*, Papermac, London.

Aron A., Melinat, E. Aron, E., Vallone, R. and Bator, R. (1997) 'The Experimental Generation of Interpersonal Closeness: A Procedure and Some Preliminary Findings', *Personality and Social Psychology Bulletin*, 23(4), 363–77.

Bateson, M.C. (1990) *Composing a Life*, Plume, New York.

Bowlby, J. (1958) 'The Nature of the Child's Tie to his Mother', *International Journal of Psychoanalysis*, 39, 350–73.

Bowlby, J. and Ainsworth, M.D.S. (1951) *Maternal Care and Mental Health*, World Health Organization, Geneva.

Cameron, J. (2012) *The Artist's Way: A Spiritual Path to Greater Creativity*, Souvenir Press, New York.

Chapman, G. (1995) *The Five Love Languages: How to Express Heartfelt Commitment to your Mate*, Northfield, Chicago.

Chodron, P. (2000) *When Things Fall Apart: Heart Advice for Difficult Times*, Shambhala, Boston.

Covey, S.R. (2015) *First Things First*, Merrill and Merrill, New York.

Deida, D. (1997) *It's a Guy Thing: An Owner's Guide for Women*, Health Communications, Deerfield Beach, FL.

Deida, D. (2004) *The Way of the Superior Man*, Sounds True, Boulder, Co.

Earnshaw, A. (1998) *Time Bombs in Families and How to Survive Them*, Spencer, Melbourne.

Euripedes (2007) *Alcestis*, edited by L.P.E. Parker, Oxford University Press, Oxford.

Feldhahn, S. (2004) *For Women Only*, Multnomah, Multnomah Falls, OR.

Feldhahn, S. and Feldhahn, J. (2006) *For Men Only: A Straightforward Guide to the Inner Lives of Women*, Multnomah, Multnomah Falls, OR.

Fredrickson, B.L. (2014) *Love 2.0: Creating Happiness and Health in Moments of Connection*, Plume, New York.

Friday, N. (1982) *My Mother Myself*, Fontana/Collins, Glasgow.

Fuller, A. (2017) The CPR Approach to Resilience, unpublished research paper available from http://www.andrewfuller.com.au.

Gable, S.L., Reis, H.T., Impett, E.A., & Asher, E.R. (2004) 'What to Do When Things Go Right? The Intrapersonal and Interpersonal Benefits of Sharing Positive Events', *Journal of Personality and Social Psychology*, 87(2), 238–45.

Gilligan, C. (1982) *In a Different Voice: Psychological Theory and Women's Development*, Harvard University Press, Cambridge, MA.

Golas, T. (1971) *The Lazy Man's Guide to Enlightenment*, Seed, Palo Alto, CA.

Gottman, J. (2011) *The Science of Trust: Emotional Attunement for Couples*, W.W. Norton, New York.

Gottman, J. and Gottman, J.S. (2016) *The Man's Guide to Women*, Rodale Books, Emmaus, PA.

Govrin, A. (2014) 'From Ethics of Care to Psychology of Care: Reconnecting Ethics of Care to Contemporary Moral Psychology', *Frontiers in Psychology*, 5, 1–10.

Hendrix, H. and Hunt, H.L. (2005) *Receiving Love: Transform Your Relationship by Letting Yourself Be Loved*, Simon and Schuster, London.

Hendry, J., Hawkes N. and Fuller, A. (2016a) *The Relationship Quotient: Creating Successful Relationships*, available from http://www.andrewfuller.com.au.

Hendry, J., Hawkes N. and Fuller, A. (2016b) *The Relationship Quotient: Creating Successful Relationships – Trust*, available from http://www.andrewfuller.com.au.

Hendry, J., Hawkes N. and Fuller, A. (2016c) *The Relationship Quotient – Forgiveness*, available from http://www.andrewfuller.com.au.

Hendry, J., Hawkes N. and Fuller, A. (2016d) *The Relationship Quotient: Creating Successful Relationships – Integrity*, available from http://www.andrewfuller.com.au.

Hendry, J., Hawkes N. and Fuller, A. (2016e) *The Relationship Quotient: Creating Successful Relationships – Hope*, available from http://www.andrewfuller.com.au.

Hendry, J., Hawkes N. and Fuller, A. (2016f) *The Relationship Quotient: Creating Successful Relationships – Compassion*, available from http://www.andrewfuller.com.au

Hudson, N.W. & Fraley, R.C. (2017) 'Adult Attachment and Perceptions of Closeness', *Personal Relationships*, 24(1), 17–26.

Johnson, R. (1991) *Transformation: Understanding the Three Levels of Masculine Consciousness*, HarperCollins, New York.

Johnson, S. (2008) *Hold Me Tight*, Piatkus, London.

Jung, C.G. (1957) *The Undiscovered Self*, Rascher, Zurich.

Lederach, J.P. (2014) *The Little Book of Conflict Transformation*, Good Books, New York.

Levine, A. and Heller, R. (2011) *Attached*, Macmillan, New York.

Livingston, G. (2005) *Too Soon Old, Too Late Smart: Thirty Things You Need to Know Now*, Hodder, Sydney.

Livingston, G. (2009) *How to Love: Who Best to Love and How Best to Love*, Hachette, Sydney.

McGinnis, A.K. (2004) *The Friendship Factor: How to Get Closer to the People You Care For*, Augsberg Books, Minneapolis, MN.

Murdock, M. (1990) *The Heroine's Journey*, Shambhala, Boston.

O'Donohue, J. (1997) *Anam Cara: A Book of Celtic Wisdom*, Bantam, London.

O'Donohue, J. (2007) *Benedictus: A Book of Blessings*, Bantam, London.

Perel, E. (2007) *Mating in Captivity: Sex, Lies and Domestic Bliss*, Hodder and Stoughton, London.

Perel, E. (2017) *The State of Affairs: Rethinking Infidelity*, Yellow Pike, London.

Porges, S.W. (2009) 'Reciprocal Influences Between Body and Brain in the Perception and Experiences of Affect: A Polyvagal Perspective', in D. Fosha, D. Seigel and M. Solomon (eds), *The Healing Power of Emotion*, W.W. Norton, New York.

Porges, S.W. (2017) *The Pocket Guide to the Polyvagal Theory: The Transformative Power of Feeling Safe*, W.W. Norton, New York.

Rapoport, A, and Chammah, A.M. (1965) *Prisoner's Dilemma: A Study in Conflict and Co-operation*, University of Michigan Press, Ann Arbor, MI.

Rogers, C. (1995) *On Becoming a Person: A Therapist's View of Psychology*, 2nd ed., Mariner Books, Wilmington, NC.

Sapolsky, R. (2004) *Why Zebras Don't Get Ulcers*, St Martin's Press, New York.

Sapolsky, R. (2017) *Behave – the Biology of Humans at Our Best and Worst*, Penguin, New York.

Seneca (1974) *Letters from a Stoic*, Penguin, Harmondsworth.

Shakespeare, W. (2017) *Much Ado About Nothing*, Pelican, London.

Skynner, R. and Cleese, J. (2009) *Families and How to Survive Them*, Random House, London.

Stark, V. (2006) *My Sister, My Self: Understanding the Sibling Relationship that Shapes Our Lives, Our Loves, and Ourselves*, McGraw Hill, New York.

Storch, M. (2007) *The Strong Woman's Desire for a Strong Man*, Finch, Sydney.

Tannen, D. (1990) *You Just Don't Understand Me*, Random House, Sydney.

Tannen, D. (2006) *You're Wearing That? Understanding Mothers and Daughters in Conversation*, Ballantyne Books, New York.

Tatkin, S. (2011) *Wired for Love: How Understanding Your Partner's Brain and Attachment Style Can Help You Defuse Conflict*, New Harbinger Press, Oakland, CA.

Tatkin, S. (2016) *Wired for Dating*, New Harbinger Press, Oakland, CA.

Tuckman, B.W. (1965) 'Development Sequence in Small Groups', *Psychological Bulletin*, 63, 384–99.

Tuckman, B.W. & Jensen, M.A.C. (1977) 'Stages of Small Group Development Revisited', *Group and Organizational Studies*, 2, 419–27.

Weiner-Davis, M. (2017) *Healing from Infidelity: The Divorce Busting Guide to Re-building your Marriage After an Affair*, Michele Weiner-Davis Training Corporation, Woodstock, IL.

Whyte, D. (2010) *The Three Marriages: Reimagining Self, Work and Relationship*, Penguin Putnam, New York.

Young-Eisendrath, P. (2000) *Women and Desire: Beyond Wanting to Be Wanted*, Piatkus, London.

Zeldin, T. (1998) *Conversation: How Talk Can Change Our Lives*, Hidden Spring, Mahwah, NJ.

ACKNOWLEDGEMENTS

Thanks to Anthony and Dianne Beardall, Brian Clarke, Lorraine Day, Rod Dungan, Lucy Fuller, Sam Fuller, Vicki Fuller, Bert Van Halen, Neil and Jane Hawkes, John Hendry, Brenda Hosking, Melissa Freedman, Kerry Howells, Joanne Jarvis, Tim Jezard, Nell Jones, Paul Jones, Ian Larsen, Ola Krupinska, Lyn Littlefield, Nitika Maharaj, Tonya Miles, Nicole Miller, Peter O'Connor, Ric Pawsey, Andrew Priestley, Diane Priestley, Margot Prior, Robert Schweitzer, Stan and Tracy Tatkin, Bob Sharples, Liz and Trevor Sheehan, Tania Smith, Vivan Thomas, David Tyson and Jessica Yehl.

Andrew Fuller began his career as a clinical psychologist in psychiatric crisis teams, working with people who were often contemplating ending their lives. The reason for their despair was frequently the loss or breakup of a relationship. Fortunately, all were helped beyond this state. This inspired Andrew to work with people to create futures they can fall in love with. He is an Honorary Fellow at the University of Melbourne.

To learn more about Andrew Fuller's work, visit www.andrewfuller.com.au, where you can access free downloads and contact information for Andrew's talks. For specific information regarding learning strengths and developing a personalised learning plan, visit www.mylearningstrengths.com. You can also follow Andrew on Facebook, for regular posts on resilience, life and relationships: 🟦/andrewfullerpsychologist